...72 he was
...phy at Oxford Univer...
Fellow of the British Academy and
Membre de l'Institut Internationale de
Philosophie. Among his most recent book
are *Questions in the Philosophy of Mind*
(1975) and *Motivated Irrationality* (1984).

Wittgenstein

David Pears

Fontana Press
An Imprint of HarperCollins*Publishers*

Fontana Press
An Imprint of HarperCollins*Publishers*
77–85 Fulham Palace Road,
Hammersmith, London W6 8JB

Published by Fontana Press, with Postscript 1985
19 18 17 16 15 14 13 12 11 10

First published in Great Britain by
Fontana 1971

Copyright © David Pears 1971, 1985

Set in Pilgrim

Printed in Great Britain by
HarperCollinsManufacturing Glasgow

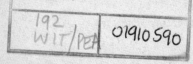

To Iris Murdoch

Contents

Preface

Some of this book appeared in a briefer form in the *New York Review of Books* on the 16th of January 1969. I would like to express my gratitude to Professor P. F. Strawson and to Mr P. L. Gardiner for reading it in its present form and suggesting improvements. The first part of the book owes much to Mr B. F. McGuinness, with whom I have discussed the early philosophy of Wittgenstein frequently and extensively.

Introduction

i. The General Character of Wittgenstein's Philosophy

Wittgenstein's philosophy is a strange product of genius, which differs in very many ways from the work of his contemporaries and predecessors. The most striking thing about his achievement is that he produced two different philosophies, one in the *Tractatus Logico-Philosophicus*, which he published in 1921, and the other in *Philosophical Investigations*, which appeared in 1953 two years after his death, and which is the most finished example of his later work. There are, of course, many lines connecting his early and his later ideas, but the differences between them are clear-cut, and their development is separated by an interval in which he gave up philosophy, taught in Austrian village schools and designed and supervised the building of a house for his sisters in Vienna.

In some periods in the history of philosophy there is general agreement about its aims and the best way of achieving them, but soon after the beginning of this century a change in the conception of philosophy began to spread from Cambridge, where it had been initiated by Russell and Moore. It was no longer seen as the direct study of thought and ideas, but, rather, as the study of them through the intermediary of language. Later, in the 1920s, Vienna became the second home of this linguistic philosophy. Wittgenstein followed the new method and made a great contribution to it, particularly in his later period. He was always aware that philosophy is a more extraordinary subject than it is commonly taken to be, and he never ceased to be preoccupied with the questions, what it is, and what it ought to be and how it ought to be done. An examination of his philosophy must, therefore, take account not only of changes of doctrine between his early and late periods, but also of changes in method.

In both periods his aim was to understand the structure and limits of thought, and his method was to study the structure and limits of language. His philosophy was a critique of language very similar in scope and purpose to Kant's critique of thought. Like Kant, he believed that philosophers often unwittingly stray beyond the limits into the kind of specious nonsense that seems to express genuine thoughts but in fact does not do so. He wanted to discover the exact location of the line dividing sense from nonsense, so that people might realize when they had reached it and stop. This is the negative side of his philosophy and it makes the first, and usually the deepest impression on his readers. But it also has another, more positive side. His purpose was not merely to formulate instructions which would save people from trying to say what cannot be said in language, but also to succeed in understanding the structure of what can be said. He believed that the only way to achieve this understanding is to plot the limits, because the limits and the structure have a common origin. The nature of language dictates both what you can and what you cannot do with it.

All Wittgenstein's doctrines are related to his idea that language has limits imposed by its internal structure. For example, in the *Tractatus* he puts forward a theory of logic deduced, like his theory of the limits of language, from his early views about the nature of propositions, and he places religion and morality beyond the limits because they do not meet the requirements of what can be said. Similarly, in *Philosophical Investigations* he rejects the theory that we might have developed a language for reporting our sensations without the help of the language in which we describe the exernal world, on the ground that such a language would fail to meet a requirement that must be met by any language.[1]

There are two main changes in Wittgenstein's doctrines between his early and his later periods. First, he abandoned the idea that the structure of reality determines the structure of language, and suggested that it is really the other way round: our language determines our view of reality, because we see things through it. So he no longer believed it to be possible to deduce the pre-existing structure of reality from the premiss that all languages have a certain common structure. This change goes very deep and involves the rejection of far more than the particular theory about reality that he propounded in the *Tractatus*. It undermines any theory that tries to base a pattern of thought, or a linguistic practice, such as logical inference, on some independent foundation in reality. If these things need any justification, it must lie within them, because there are no independent points of support outside them. That kind of objectivism is an illusion, produced, no doubt, by the unreassuring character of the true explanation, which is that any support that is needed comes from the centre, man himself.

The second main doctrinal change is in Wittgenstein's theory of language. In the *Tractatus* he had argued that all languages have a uniform logical structure, which does not necessarily show on the surface, but which can be disclosed by philosophical analysis. The differences between linguistic forms seemed to him to be superficial variations on a single theme, dictated by logic. Early in his second period of philosophical activity he came round to the diametrically opposite view. The diversification of linguistic forms, he now thought, actually reveals the deep structure of lan-

1. In this example the connection with the limits of language is more complicated than it appears to be: it is the philosophical theory that there might have been such a language for sensations which deviates into nonsense, because it misapplies the word 'language'. See Chapter 8.

guage, which is not at all what he had taken it to be. Language has no common essence, or at least, if it has one, it is a minimal one, which does not explain the connections between its various forms. They are connected with one another in a more elusive way, like games, or like the faces of people belonging to the same family.

This new theory of language is the key to the understanding of Wittgenstein's later philosophy, because it led to a radical change in his method. The puzzling thing about his later philosophy is that it is so piecemeal. The *Tractatus* is a continuous treatise, with a clear aim and a fairly clear way of achieving it: the essential nature of language must be isolated and described so that its structure and limits may be determined. But in *Philosophical Investigations* it is easier to get lost, because, although it was put together in the same way—it is a series of remarks selected from notebooks and arranged according to their subject-matter—it has no master plan. There is the same concern with the structure and limits of language, but they are no longer deduced from a single comprehensive theory. They are extracted bit by bit from a mass of inter-related linguistic material. The result is a new kind of philosophical work which contains no sweeping generalization and remarkably little categorical assertion. It is full of perfectly ordinary detailed descriptions of language, which are presented dialectically in a way that invites the reader to take part in the dialogue.

It would have been difficult for Wittgenstein merely to emend the *Tractatus* because it is a very finished piece of work. It was much admired by Russell, with whom he had worked in Cambridge just before the 1914 war, and it made a great impression on the philosophers of the Vienna Circle. Its subsequent influence on linguistic philosophy was strong, but exerted from a distance, because it is very abstract and sublime and does not often descend to the details of philosophical problems.

After the publication of the *Tractatus* Wittgenstein turned from philosophy to schoolteaching and architecture. He spent two years on the house in Vienna, which, according to Von Wright, 'is his work down to the smallest detail, and is highly characteristic of its creator. It is free from all decoration and marked by a severe exactitude in measure and proportion. Its beauty is of the same simple and static kind that belongs to the sentences of the *Tractatus*'.[2] The interval separating his two periods of philosophical activity ended in 1929, when he returned to Cambridge, first as a research student and then in the following year as a fellow of Trinity College. He had come back to philosophy gradually. Frank Ramsey, who produced the first English translation of the *Tractatus* with C. K. Ogden, had established contact with him in Austria in 1923, and in 1927 Moritz Schlick had persuaded him to meet two other members of the Vienna Circle, Rudolf Carnap and Friedrich Waismann, and discuss philosophy with them. They wanted to know how the exceedingly abstract doctrines of the *Tractatus* were to be worked out in detail and applied.

Wittgenstein had thought that the *Tractatus* gave the key to the final solution of the problems of philosophy. When he realized that it was based on an erroneous theory of language, he had to make a fresh, but not completely different start. Instead of deducing the structure and limits of language from an abstract logical theory, he would try to discover them through an empirical investigation. Language is a part of human life and it should be examined in that setting with all its complexities of form and function.

In Cambridge Wittgenstein taught philosophy in an unusual way, which has been described by Norman Malcolm in his *Memoir*.[3] His lectures were given to small audiences,

2. G. H. Von Wright: *Biographical Sketch*, p. 11, in *Ludwig Wittgenstein, A Memoir* by Norman Malcolm, with a *Biographical Sketch* by Georg Henrik von Wright, Oxford University Press, 1958.

3. Loc. cit., pp. 23–9.

because he did not allow people to attend sporadically or for a short time, and they were drawn from his thoughts about the problems with which he was wrestling at the time and delivered without notes and with very little preparation for the occasion. They were as unlike ordinary lectures as *Philosophical Investigations* is unlike an ordinary book. He was really thinking aloud, and he might succeed in pushing his investigation of a problem beyond the point that he had reached in his meditations outside the lecture room, so that his audience would witness the difficult, and sometimes painful emergence of his new ideas. They also took part in the process, because he drew them into the discussion and dealt with their objections. He conducted the meetings with deep seriousness and relentless determination never to be satisfied with incomplete or superficial solutions and he made very great demands both on his audience and on himself.

It was not only the force of Wittgenstein's intellect and personality that produced the strange shared intensity of these meetings. There was also a peculiar feature of his later method which distinguished his philosophy from all previous philosophy and gave it an almost confessional character. He regarded his new work on the structure and limits of language as a continuous struggle against the bewitchment of the intellect. Philosophical theories are a product of the imagination, and they offer us simple, but seemingly profound pictures, which blind us to the actual complexities of language. The new philosophy is an organized resistance to this enchantment, and its method is always to bring us back to the linguistic phenomena, with which we are perfectly familiar, but which we cannot keep in focus when we philosophize in the old way. Wittgenstein compared this method to the treatment of an illness. But if addiction to philosophical theories is like an illness, it is a necessary illness, because, without it, the empirical investigation of language would lose its point. You have to experience the temptation to misconstrue language before you can achieve philosophical understanding. The limit of language is not a single, continuous boundary which, when it has once been pointed out, can be recognized as impassable, but a maze of boundaries which can be understood only by those who have felt the urge to cross them, have made the attempt and have been forced back.

Wittgenstein was aware that his new philosophy might well appear to be completely different from the subject studied by his predecessors and even from the subject discussed in the *Tractatus*. But there are strong and deep connections linking his later to his earlier work, and linking that to the main tradition of western thought. The only way to understand his philosophy is to go back into the past and to trace these lines of development, with particular attention to the relationship between his philosophy and traditional metaphysics.

ii. Pre-Critical Philosophy

People who want to know what philosophy is are often surprised that philosophers do not find it at all easy to tell them. The question would be a simple one, if it were possible to pin philosophy down by specifying its subject-matter. But though this kind of answer would work for philology or for psychology, it would not work for philosophy, because philosophy ranges over so many subjects. There is the philosophy of religion, but there is also the philosophy of science; or, to name a pair which are more closely connected with one another, there is moral philosophy and the philosophy of mind. But these are only a few examples. Any subject of sufficient generality and importance has a branch of philosophy devoted to it. So it is no good using subject-matter as a clue to the nature of philosophy.

The alternative is to describe the way in which philosophy treats whatever subject comes its way. This must be the right kind of answer to the question, because the distinctive mark of philosophy can hardly be its omnivorousness. A philosopher is not a man of universal knowledge, nor is a philosophical book a compendium which would make it unnecessary to buy other books, unless someone happened to want further details. So there must be something distinctive about the way in which philosophers go to work, about their method and the kind of thinking that they practise, and, therefore, presumably about the character of their results.

But though this must be the right way of dealing with the question, it is, as every student of philosophy soon discovers, not at all easy to get a really convincing answer of this kind. Teachers of philosophy naturally tend to base their descriptions of the subject on their own method and on the character of the results at which they themselves aim. They may claim that their way of doing philosophy is revolutionary, or they may allow more generously that earlier philosophers often worked on the same lines without quite realizing it. An answer arrived at in this way may well have some truth in it, but it will be only too obvious that it is largely an accident of time and place. A quick glance at the way in which philosophy is done in different parts of the world today is enough to dispel any illusion of unanimity about its general nature and anyone who looks back into its history will find a bewildering variety of different conceptions of it. Of course, nobody ought to be surprised to find disputes between philosophers who share the same general conception of what they are doing. That happens in other subjects too. But disagreement about the nature of philosophy itself is more surprising. Perhaps the question 'What is philosophy?' is more like the question 'What is art?'. Certainly the history of science has not thrown up such diverse conceptions of the nature of scientific thought.

In the last fifty years there has been more controversy about the nature of philosophy than in any earlier period in the history of western thought. This is an important fact which complicates the assessment of Wittgenstein's achievement. For often when people give differing estimates of his achievement, the explanation is that they are starting from divergent conceptions of what philosophy is. Russell, for example, has a low opinion of Wittgenstein's second book, *Philosophical Investigations*, while others regard it as a work of genius. The divergence between these two assessments evidently goes back to the question what standard ought to be used. For Russell condemns *Philosophical Investigations* not because it fails in the right kind of endeavour, but because, according to him, the endeavour has nothing to do with philosophy. He thinks that, unlike the *Tractatus Logico-Philosophicus*, it is a trivial investigation of language, in no way connected with the investigation of logic, knowledge and reality which he regards as the proper task of philosophy.[4]

The predicament is a familiar one, because it is not confined to the history of ideas, but occurs in many places where criticism and evaluation are needed. Something has to be measured, but when we set about the task, we find that the first thing to be done is to select the right scale of measurement. But what is the right scale? If there is no objective way of arriving at the answer to this question, how are we to start? It would be harsh to judge a work by some totally alien standard, but it would be silly to allow it to dictate the standard to be used simply with a view to its own success. Everything is the size that it is, and extreme tolerance would end in tautology and banality.

However, at least in the history of philosophy the predicament is not quite as difficult as it appears to be. There are really two things which reduce the difficulty in this

4. Bertrand Russell: *My Philosophical Development*, pp. 216-17, Allen and Unwin, 1959.

area. First, there is something common to the various endeavours which have claimed the title 'philosophy'. Secondly, the different ways in which the rival claimants have developed from their common origin can be described and to some extent justified. So when they try to shout each other down, we need not listen. We can ignore the bedlam, and attain some degree of objectivity by tracing the divergent ways in which they have developed from a single starting point.

What, then, is it that different conceptions of philosophy have in common? It is hardly likely that it will be anything that can be described very specifically. Perhaps in the end it will only be possible to characterize it negatively. Plato, Schopenhauer and many other philosophers have said that the origin of philosophy is a kind of wonder or refusal to take things for granted. But though this is true, it cannot be the whole truth, because it needs to be made more specific. Science too starts from the same feeling and the same intellectual attitude, but philosophy is not science. So what differentiates them?

Part of the answer to this question is that they are distinguished by the methods that they use. Science uses observation and experiment, but philosophy uses neither. But though this too is true, it is an entirely negative description of the method of philosophy, and it leaves too much in darkness. Is philosophy, then, armchair science? Does the philosopher achieve by pure thought results which the scientist can achieve only by toiling in his laboratory? But that is an absurd suggestion. There must also be a difference between the results at which each of them aims. The kind of understanding which the philosopher seeks must differ from the kind of understanding sought by the scientist. But what is the difference?

At this point we might be advised to give up the search for a distinctive common factor. For it might well seem that the question 'What is philosophy?' does not have a single answer which would capture the essence of all the various manifestations of the philosophical spirit. Any single differentiating characteristic which might be suggested would be either inappropriate to certain cases, or else too vaguely specified to be at all informative.

However, though this dilemma exactly locates the difficulty of characterizing philosophy, there is a way between its two horns. We can say that the kind of understanding sought by philosophers goes beyond the kind of understanding sought by scientists. But though this too is true, it is vague, and, however positive it may sound, it really only gives a negative characterization of philosophy, since it does not tell us where a thinker who ventured beyond the limits of science would go. All that it really tells us is that he would not work within those limits. It also suffers from another inadequacy: it attempts to relate philosophical thought to scientific thought, but it does not say anything about the ways in which it is related to other modes of thought.

Archimedes said that he could move the world, if he could find a point in space which would serve as the fulcrum for a sufficiently long lever. His idea can be used as an image to illustrate the origin of philosophy. Philosophy originates in the desire to transcend the world of human thought and experience, in order to find some point of vantage from which it can be seen as a whole. This enterprise would require an unusual intellectual apparatus. For the world of human thought and experience must not only be seen, but also apprehended and described: and that creates two needs, the need for a set of ideas which could be applied universally, and the need for a master language to express those ideas. But this would only be the first stage. The ultimate purpose is not merely to describe, but also to explain and to understand, and the understanding that is sought is not at all the sort of thing that counts as understanding in the sublunary world. The aim is higher, and the desired understanding more synoptic. For example, the question, why a particular species of animal exists, is answerable by zoology, but the question, why anything at all exists, cannot be answered by any science. Or, to take an example from logic, the question, whether a particular scientific argument is valid, can be settled by reference to the accepted standards of inductive validity, but the question, whether the standards themselves ought to be accepted, cannot be settled in any such way.

It is natural to characterize this enterprise by relating it to science. For science is organized factual knowledge, and metaphysical philosophers, who have actually tried to carry out the enterprise, have always used the system of factual knowledge as their model. What other usable model is there? At the same time they have nearly always been aware of the differences between philosophy and science. One difference, which has already been mentioned, is that factual knowledge is based on observation and experiment, but philosophy is not. Another, connected difference is that factual statements are at best only contingently true, because any matter of fact might have been other than it is, whereas philosophical statements are supposed to be necessarily true. So between philosophy and factual knowledge there is a dividing line as well as an affinity.

This dividing line has always been one of the most important features on the map of western ideas. Its importance has been especially obvious since the Renaissance and the development of science, and there have been many controversies about its exact location. However, there are places where its location is not in doubt, and one very natural way of explaining what philosophy is would be to select one of these places, and to show how a question ceases to be scientific and becomes philosophical when it is pushed across the line. Thus the question, 'Why does this species exist?', is clearly scientific, but the question 'Why does anything at all exist?' is equally clearly on the other side of the line, and so belongs to philosophy. Yet when a question crosses this line it still retains its affinity with science. In fact, it may try to retain too much of it.

So the reason for choosing this approach to the question, what philosophy is, can be put in the form of a subtraction sum. When we watch factual questions being transformed into philosophical questions, we see that something is subtracted from their character, but also that something else remains the same.

But when philosophy is approached from this direction, it presents only one of its aspects. Maybe the first and most important thing is to see how it is related to factual knowledge, but it is also necessary to see how it is related to other modes of thought and other interests. Understanding is sometimes sought for its own sake, but the search has often had a further end in view. The question, why the standards of inductive argument should be accepted, hints at the possibility of scepticism, but it is really a question about the structure of the system of factual knowledge, and in this case understanding is desired for its own sake. But the question, why the standards of morality should be accepted, has a very different character underneath the similarity of form. For the feelings which prompt this question may be genuine uncertainty and doubt, and not the paper doubt of the sceptic about induction. In this case it is not even clear which standards are the best candidates for acceptance, and the moral philosopher is not merely being asked to justify a system which is agreed by all rational human beings. The solution to this problem affects our lives, and the feeling which leads us across the line which divides morality from philosophy need not be wonder at something given, or at least taken : it may be genuine uncertainty what, if anything, is there. Or, to choose another example, whatever good may be, evil, pain and death present problems of another, different kind.

But from whatever direction philosophy is approached,

the transition always has the same character. The line enclosing all that we have been taught, however rightly, to accept, is crossed, and the most elementary things become a source of wonder. Although this movement of thought is sometimes a sceptical one, that is by no means always so. What is always the case is that philosophy seeks a wider view, and an understanding which goes beyond what counts as understanding in any other discipline. This is very evidently true of metaphysical philosophy, but it is also true, in a different and less obvious way, of contemporary linguistic philosophy. For example, a detailed analysis of moral judgements, however narrowly focused it may seem to be, will really be comparative, because it will try to place moral judgements in relation to other types of judgement, and in so doing it will raise questions which reach beyond the limits of morality.

So far, the emphasis has been on what is common to the varieties of philosophical thought. Their point of origin has been located, and the general direction in which they move has been indicated. Both these things have been done vaguely and even negatively, but in spite of that there has already been some exaggeration of the common factor. What has been exaggerated is not the unity of philosophy's origin, because, as a matter of historical fact, it did originate in the way described under the pressure of those feelings, and even today students of philosophy recapitulate at least part of the evolution of the subject in their own thoughts about it. It is the unity of aim that has been exaggerated. For part of the description of the results at which philosophers aim fits metaphysical philosophy better than it fits the other varieties. This exaggeration must now be corrected, but it will also be justified to some extent. The correction will take the form of a description of the results which other varieties of philosophy try to achieve. The justification will be that the exaggeration draws attention to a deeper unity of aim which is sometimes missed by those who emphasize, however rightly, the differences between the various ways of doing philosophy.

iii. Critical Philosophy

There are many ways of distinguishing and classifying types of philosophy, but there is one distinction which, for the present purpose, is more important than any other, the distinction between metaphysical philosophy and critical philosophy. The word 'metaphysics' has several shades of meaning, but, when Kant drew this distinction in the eighteenth century, he meant 'speculative metaphysics', and he was suggesting a reform. He believed that a thorough critical examination of the scope and limits of human thought would show that the great systems of speculative metaphysics were founded on nothing. If there had been a point in space which would serve as a fulcrum for Archimedes' lever, he could have moved the world. If there had been a point of vantage and a suitable set of ideas, the speculative metaphysician could have seen the world of human thought and experience from the outside, and he could have written a book which placed it in some larger system. But, according to Kant, this sort of transcendence cannot be achieved. For when philosophy tries to go beyond all possible experience, and at the same time tries to retain the outlook of experience, there is nowhere for it to go. So the proper task of philosophy is a systematic criticism of human thought which would demonstrate the impossibility of metaphysical speculation. Thinking becomes truly philosophical when it turns back and examines itself.

It is the negative aspect of critical philosophy which makes the first, and sometimes the most lasting impression. Something has been lost, and, as often happens when there is a revolutionary change in the way in which philosophy is conceived, what has been lost seems to be more than it really is. A similar impression was made in this century by linguistic philosophy, which is another species of critical philosophy. A sudden change makes it difficult to see the underlying continuity, or, at least, difficult to see it at the time. A similar difficulty has often been felt in the history of art.

Part of Kant's case against speculative metaphysics was not really new, and could never be contested once it had been stated clearly. For it cannot very well be denied that there is some equivocation in the suggestion that philosophy might go beyond all possible experience and still retain the outlook of experience. 'All' really does mean 'all'. So speculative metaphysicians were ready with the defence that, though their statments sounded like statements of contingent fact, they were not really meant in that way. Nevertheless, Kant was right to press this simple criticism, because it is so difficult to extirpate the idea that philosophy is some sort of extension of the system of factual knowledge. A brief rejection of this idea is never enough. It is necessary to demonstrate in a systematic way that, whenever thinking becomes philosophical, it loses almost all its affinity with science. So Kant developed his simple criticism in detail, concentrating on those parts of the line between science and philosophy which had been crossed most frequently by his predecessors without full awareness of what the crossing involved. For example, the concept of a cause had often been taken beyond the bounds of factual knowledge, to be used in the rarefied atmosphere of speculative cosmology, and Kant tried to show that it is impossible to use it there or anywhere else where there is no material to which it can be applied.

But Kant's case against speculative metaphysics is more elaborate than this. It is impossible to follow all its ramifications here, but there is one argument of his which ought to be mentioned. He had to deal with the claim that metaphysical statements are not statements of contingent facts but necessary truths. For example, a speculative cosmologist might claim that it is a necessary truth that there is a first cause. Kant used an elaborate argument against this claim. He observed that some necessary truths are empty tautologies, but that the supposed necessary truths of transcendent metaphysics are about matters of substance: to put his point in technical terms, they are synthetic necessary truths. He then argued that any attempt to prove the necessity of a metaphysical thesis of this kind could be met by an equally plausible proof of the opposite thesis. If this kind of metaphysical reasoning had any force, it would show not only that there must be a first cause, but also that there cannot be a first cause. This kind of contradiction he took as a sure sign that a concept had been carried beyond the limits of its proper use. He allowed that it is possible to establish the substantial necessary truth that every event has a cause, but he argued that this is a necessity which holds only within the bounds of factual knowledge, and that there is nothing to support it in the thin air beyond.

This kind of argument was new, and it is more important and more controversial than the simple criticism of speculative metaphysics which was mentioned first. It takes account of the fact that metaphysical speculation was not supposed to be based on an extrasensory way of apprehending contingent truths. So, starting from a simple foundation Kant developed an elaborate critique of the concept of necessity. But here we need not concern ourselves with the details of his system. It has to be described only so far as is necessary to establish the general character of critical philosophy and its connections with the past.

When human thought turns around and examines itself, where does the investigation start? And how does it proceed? The short answer to the first question is that there are two forms in which the data to be investigated may be presented. They may be presented in a psychological form, as ideas, thoughts and modes of thought: or they may be presented in a linguistic form, as words, sentences and types of discourse. Kant's critique starts from data of the first kind, and the second wave of critical philosophy, the logico-analytic movement of this century, starts from data of the second kind.

It is easy to see why there is this choice of starting point. The reason is that it does not make any fundamental difference which alternative is chosen, because a significant sentence must express a thought, and a genuine thought must be expressible in words. However, the choice of starting point does determine the form of the subsequent inquiry, and this leads to an important consequential difference. Philosophy is not a science, but it has always existed rather ambiguously on the fringe of science. So when it is conceived as the direct investigation of thought, it is necessary to draw a firm line between it and psychology, and when it is conceived as the investigation of thought through the intermediary of language, it is necessary to draw a firm line between it and the science of linguistics.

How are these lines to be drawn? If philosophy cannot move beyond other modes of thought into an area of its own, how will it maintain its independence? In particular, if it cannot transcend science in this way, will it not be absorbed into one of the sciences, perhaps into psychology or perhaps into linguistics? No doubt it is true that it is not distinguished by its subject matter, but this admission leaves it in a very precarious position. What, if anything, does distinguish it?

One way of working out answers to these questions is to go back to the critical philosophy of the eighteenth century, and to examine it more thoroughly. So far, only the negative side of Kant's *Critique of Pure Reason* has been described, but it is not a purely destructive piece of work. In fact, it is not really destructive at all. For Kant allows that the ideas of speculative metaphysics have a proper function, and what he attacks is really only the attempt to make them perform another function, which they cannot perform. Their proper function, according to him, is to serve as notional points of reference, which lie outside the system of factual knowledge, and so can be used to orient it. They are not parts of the system, but ideals to which it approximates. For example, a single theory, in which everything would find a place and be explained, is neither necessary nor possible, but the idea of such a theory serves as a guide for the theories which we do construct. It goes too far, but it goes too far in the right direction. The mistake, Kant thought, is to suppose that such metaphysical ideas have an objective basis outside the system of factual knowledge, instead of recognizing them for what they are, purely notional prolongations of lines which guide the development of human thought. It is as if a diagram were misread, because a point, which functioned only in its geometrical construction, was taken to represent something.

Here, then, is one place at which it can be seen that Kant's critical revolution did not change the whole nature of philosophy. Certainly, philosophy never was a science with a field of its own, and this section of the line which separates it from science is fairly easy to draw. But the feelings and aspirations which sent it in that direction were not completely mistaken. The wonder and the sense of a totality were right. What was wrong was the direction that they made philosophy take, however natural it seemed at the time. So there was no question of destroying the force behind philosophical thinking. What was required was that the resultant movement should be deflected in the right direction.

A similar attitude to the great metaphysical systems of the past can be found in some of the linguistic philosophy of this century. Of course, when this philosophy takes the form of positivism, the attitude is usually intolerant and destructive. But in the writings of many linguistic philosophers, and conspicuously in Wittgenstein's work, the treatment of metaphysics is sympathetic and understanding. It is true that Wittgenstein's attitude to metaphysical thinking is not the same as Kant's and the differences will be described later. But they have this much in common: both regard it as a natural and inevitable transgressor, and both think that much can be learned from its excesses.

But this sort of treatment may not concede very much. The great philosophy of the past might become a sort of jester at the court of critical philosophy, with a repertoire of instructive parodies and pathetically unattainable ideals. But though the tolerance which critical philosophers show towards metaphysics does sometimes have this condescending air, there is more to it than that. After all, much depends on what they learn from it, and on how what they learn is related to their own philosophy.

There is, in any case, something else which remained constant through the change, something which is perhaps less obvious but more important. When thought turns back and examines itself, instead of examining its own shadows in the void, there is not really any change of subject. There is, of course, a revolutionary change in the conception of it, which moves through one hundred and eighty degrees, but the subject itself, philosophy, remains the same. Suppose, for example, that Kant was right in regarding causality not as an objective feature of reality, but as a kind of grid imposed on reality by the mind which views it: even so, much of the philosophical investigation of causality would remain unaltered. This may seem incredible, because, if a scientist became convinced that what he saw through his microscope was an effect of a flaw in the lens, he would start all over again. But the analogy is imperfect at the essential point. A microscope yields one set of observations, whereas what comes through the lens of the mind is the totality of human experience. So in this case there is no possibility of sidestepping and no independent check, and the very idea, that this lens might be flawed, seems to be empty. When the field is extended to the limit, there does not seem to be any possibility of discovering that thought and reality might fail to fit one another.

Then which of the two is dominant? Which gives the harmonious system the character that it has? Did reality mould thought, or was thought already endowed with characteristics of its own? There is no need to go any further into Kant's complicated solution to this problem, because the main point of critical philosophy is unaffected by it. Whatever the explanation, the fact is that in certain general ways thought and reality must fit one another. So critical philosophy has not really changed the subject. The self-examination of thought is still an investigation of reality. The investigation has merely lost its directness because it has lost its claim to a field of its own. But the same feelings are still at work. The difference is that the sense of wonder is now directed at certain features of our own thinking, and the understanding which is sought is understanding of our own conceptual system.

It is easy to exaggerate sameness and differences. But if we take our stand at this deeper level of continuity, the critical revolution in philosophy can be seen as a movement near the surface. However, this description of the change would be a philosopher's description of it. There is also another point of view, outside philosophy, from which the change seems greater. In order to work our way round to this other point of view, we must first draw a distinction which is implicit in the account already given of Kant's philosophy. For the question really is, how great an effect is produced when philosophy is centred on man, and this question can be answered only if we distinguish between different modes of thought, and assess the effect of the shift towards anthropocentrism on each of them separately.

Kant's treatment of causality is a clear illustration of the shift towards anthropocentrism. Formerly causality had been regarded as an objective feature of reality, and then Kant treated it as a projection of the human mind. Hume had done this too, but in a different way. Here it is important to observe that there are, according to Kant, two distinct kinds of projection. Speculative metaphysics merely examines the shadows of its own ideas in the void, because it projects them too far, and, therefore, onto nothing. But ordinary factual thinking and science use a different kind of projection. For they operate within the bounds of possible experience, and so they have something onto which to project their ideas. They have what is given in experience. Now, if pure philosophy were our only concern, we could say that, when Kant put man at the centre of his system, this 'Copernican revolution', as he called it, did not make any really fundamental change. Certainly, it vastly extended the scope of the idea that the mind may create what it is usually supposed to discover. But there was no general condemnation of mental projections. Only projections into the void were condemned, and projections on to genuine and appropriate material became the proper study of philosophy.

When we carry this distinction forward into this century and apply it to linguistic philosophy, we get a roughly similar result. If words are applied to genuine and appropriate material, they make sense: if not, they are, as Wittgenstein puts it, idle cogs in the machine. But it would be strange to argue that, because language is a creation of the human mind, it cannot be a guide to the general features of reality.

However, though this may be a balanced account of the way in which pure philosophy is affected by the shift towards anthropocentrism, there is more to be said from another point of view. When philosophy seemed to reach out into a field of its own, that field included not only speculative metaphysics but also religion and morality, and these two subjects came through the critical revolution in a very different way. Kant's intention was to preserve them by dissociating them from the system of factual knowledge. But in their case the dissociation could hardly be carried out in the way in which it had been carried out for philosophy. Philosophy had become the critique of other modes of thought, including scientific thought. But, of course, neither science nor religion nor morality could be regarded as critiques of further modes of thought. All three are on the ground level, and all three would claim to be directly based on material of their own. But religion and morality are evidently not based on the same kind of material as science. In fact, according to Kant, any form of association between them and science would be disastrous to them. For example, he rejected Hume's psychological theory that morality is simply based on widespread human feelings, because it seemed to him to make moral beliefs dangerously subjective; and he condemned the attempt to find a transcendent basis for religion, because he believed that the old arguments for the existence of God took the concepts of science beyond their proper limits and so collapsed in contradictions.

What place then could be found for religion and morality? On what basis may we claim that God exists, or that human souls are immortal, or that human wills are free? Kant's answer was that, though these central truths cannot be known, they are postulates which we have to make when we reflect on our moral life and thought. So the speculative metaphysicians who tried to establish them on theoretical grounds were mistaken. But we are not therefore left without any resource, because when we look within ourselves, and examine our moral thinking rather than our scientific thinking, we can, in some way, see beyond the limits of the system of factual knowledge. There is no need to try to assess the merits of this particular solution, because all that is required here is a general description of the predicament, and of the possible reactions to it. The predicament is often supposed to have been produced by the second wave of critical philosophy in this century. But in fact it is a common feature of all critical philosophy. Anthropocentrism leaves religion and morality in an exposed position, and it produces this effect both when it takes a psychological form, as it did in the eighteenth century, and when it takes a linguistic form, as it has done in this century.

One way of seeing how exposed this position is would be to look at the other possibilities which lie on either side of Kant's solution to the problem. On one side there is the pseudo-scientific treatment, against which he obviously reacted. But on the other side there is the kind of positivism which can be found in Hume's theory of morality, against which he reacted less obviously and in a less easily intelligible way. This type of positivism is quite different from the much better known destructive type. The general message of positivism is that there is no knowledge but scientific knowledge, and even if this is not a true thesis, it can have a salutary effect in philosophy. For when philosophy takes the form of speculative metaphysics, it pretends to be a kind of super science, and positivism refuses to allow it this false identity, and forces it out into the open where its ambiguous character can be dissected. But when this restrictive theory of knowledge is applied to religion and morality, it produces a crisis. Its application to these subjects may, of course, lead to the total rejection of them, on the ground that there is nothing whatsoever in them. This is the destructive form of positivism, and it is what people usually have in mind when they use the word 'positivist'. But there is also the possibility of applying it to these subjects in another, more interesting way. The answer to the question, what their basis is, may take a psychological or anthropological form: 'That is how people are.'

Hume's theory of morality is an example of this subtle form of positivism. It is anthropocentric, but not sceptical, because the suggestion is that human nature provides a sufficiently firm basis for morality.

Three of these four solutions to the problem reappear in the linguistic philosophy of this century. Naturally, the pseudo-scientific solution is scarcely to be found there. Of the remaining three the best known is the destructive solution offered by some logical positivists: religion and morality are nonsense. But it must be observed that even this thesis, contrary to popular belief, does not always amount to a complete rejection of religion and morality, because there are shades of sense and nonsense, and leniency is often shown to morality. However, this is a crude thesis, and its interest lies in its footnotes. The Kantian solution, or rather a late romantic development of it, is to be found in Wittgenstein's *Tractatus Logico-Philosophicus*: the central truths of religion and morality cannot be caught in the network of language, but they can be apprehended through it, and so the way to see beyond the limits of factual discourse is not to look beyond them, but to look back on the world of facts and see it as a whole. In his later work Wittgenstein moves towards a different solution, which is closely related to Hume's subtle kind of positivism. The transcendental treatment of religion and morality has gone, and its place has been taken by a kind of linguistic naturalism: there are these forms of human life and thought, and, since they have no independent basis outside themselves, a request for their justification can be met only by a careful description of the language in which they find expression, and of its place in our lives. If this were all, the solution would be a familiar one. But set in the context of his later philosophy, it has an unusual effect: for he treats scientific argument and even logic in the same levelling way.

The history of critical philosophy is the history of the partition of a heritage. When the division and realignment are observed from a point outside the movement, the most conspicuous problem is, no doubt, the resettlement of religion and morality. But when we looked closely at the placing of philosophy itself, we saw that here too there is a problem of demarcation. Critical philosophy condemns speculative metaphysics on the ground that it is an impossible extension of scientific thinking, but, when it presents this case, it is apt to put itself in jeopardy. Its ambition is to draw a line around the system of factual knowledge, and its method is to develop a systematic critique of human thought, but, whichever form this critique takes, there is a danger that it will be absorbed into one of the sciences. If it takes a psychological form, how will it draw the line between itself and psychology? And if it takes a linguistic form, how will it draw the line between itself and linguistics?

Critical philosophy has always been a very self-conscious movement of thought, because it starts from the realization that philosophy cannot take its own position for granted. If philosophy studies language, how will it maintain its independence from linguistics? This is the modern form of the problem. Now there are various possible solutions to it, but there is no need to try to decide between them here. All that is needed is a broad picture of the various developments of linguistic philosophy.

The difficulty is that any study of language, whether it be philosophical or scientific, will certainly involve the noting of facts, and will probably involve the construction of theories. When the problem is set out in this way, it seems that the difference between the two investigations must lie in the kind of theory which is sought. For example, in the science of linguistics, Chomsky seeks a theory which will explain the proliferation of grammatical forms by tracing them back to a small set of fundamental structures. But, though the theory of language, which Wittgenstein developed in the *Tractatus*, was also very general and systematic, there are differences which are sufficient to make it a philosophical, rather than a scientific theory. Its aim was not to explain how what has been done was done, but, rather, to set a limit to what can be done. It was a critical attempt to fix the bounds of any possible development of language, and, as such, it was not concerned with what is humanly possible, or with the limitations imposed by the structure of the human brain. Wittgenstein wanted to plot the absolute limits of language, just as Kant wanted to plot the absolute limits of thought.

But though this programme is clearly differentiated from any scientific programme, it is not so easy to understand how it could possibly be carried out. Wittgenstein knew that results of such range and scope could never be achieved by the methods of science, and he based his early theory of language on a very general intuition about the essential nature of propositions. His later philosophy starts from the realization that this is not a possible alternative, because it gives the theory precisely the metaphysical character which critical philosophy was supposed to eliminate. He was aware of this consequence when he was developing the theory, but he had not yet come to take a pessimistic view of its implications. At that time he believed that his theory of language was a good metaphysical theory. It could not be true, because, according to him, metaphysical theories are never true. They are attempts to say what can be shown, but cannot be said, and only what can be said can be true. But a metaphysical theory may be good, because the point which it mistakenly tries to express in factual propositions may be a valid one. At the time of writing the *Tractatus* he believed that in this sense his early theory of language was a good metaphysical theory. His later abandonment of that belief reopened the question, what distinguishes the method and results of philosophy from the method and results of science. What are the other possible answers to this question?

Wittgenstein's second answer to it was that the critique of language must be applied to itself. The critique condemns any attempt to take language beyond the proper limits of its application, on a sort of holiday. But if the critique is based on a speculative theory about the essence of language, the first thing that it should do is to set itself in order, and stop the verbal Saturnalia in its own house. But how is this to be done? Wittgenstein's new idea was that the correct method would be to avoid theorizing about language, and to concentrate on assembling facts about language. This sounds like a rudimentary kind of scientific procedure, arrested at its first stage, and shorn of everything which would give it interest. But really it is something very different. The idea is that in philosophy to theorize is to falsify, and the facts about language are offered as a corrective. Always we are to be brought back from generalities to the particular case, and this retrieval is required not only when we stray into the kind of theory which was always condemned by critical philosophy, but also when we stray into the kind of theory which critical philosophy was only too ready to offer as a substitute. Philosophy, according to this new view, is more like an art than a science. It has turned back from the quest for some more general and inclusive system, and the sense of wonder now finds its object and its satisfaction in the nuances of the particular case. These can be exhibited by careful collocations of examples, but they cannot be caught in any system of classification. If mystery is what is not amenable to scientific treatment, the source of the mysterious character of language is no longer its deep essence: it is everywhere, and it is on the surface.

Wittgenstein's two views of linguistic philosophy are not the only two, though perhaps they are the only two which draw a really firm line between philosophy and science. In order to put his views in their setting, there is no need for an account of all the different ways in which linguistic philosophy has been done. But there is one other way of doing it which must be mentioned, because it is the most important alternative to Wittgenstein's philosophy in either of its two forms. When he moved from his first to his second view of philosophy, he deliberately stepped across a third possibility. Might not philosophy abandon its claim to an intuitive apprehension of the essential nature of language without at the same time abandoning any attempt to theorize? This possibility has been explored by Russell, Carnap, Quine, Strawson and many others. It is from this standpoint that Russell's criticisms of Wittgenstein were made. In his introduction to the first edition of Wittgenstein's *Tractatus*, Russell expressed doubts about his mystical attitude to language, and in the criticism of his later work, which has already been mentioned, one of his complaints was that the new method leads to completely unsystematic results.

Why should linguistic philosophy not be systematic? What is wrong with the suggestion that philosophy ought to theorize about language in a way that would reveal the general nature of the material to which language is applied? It is not universally true that to generalize is to falsify. So why should it be true in this case? In fact, it is arguable that Wittgenstein's later philosophy does not, and cannot, avoid implicit generalizations. For if citing a fact about language corrects a false generalization, it surely must also suggest truer ones. Wittgenstein's later thought always seems to move from philosophical generalizations to the facts which falsify them. But can the movement stop abruptly there? No doubt, the truth in philosophy is very complex, but complexity is not unanalysable uniqueness.

There is no need to develop the case for systematic linguistic philosophy, which in one form or another is at the present time the chief rival of Wittgensteinian philosophy, but there are two points about it which ought to be added. First, if critical philosophy is done in a systematic way, it will come closer to science both in its methods and in the general form of its results. It is true that the line dividing philosophy from science will not be obliterated. For there will still be something fundamental which distinguishes them from one another, and, incidentally, links philosophy with its own past: systematic critical philosophy is interested in facts about language not because they are as they are, but because it sees them as exemplifications of certain possibilities taken from a range restricted by certain necessities. For instance, logic sets an absolute limit to the development and use of language. Or, to take another different kind of case, it is arguable that any language which allows the ascription of sensations and thoughts to persons will necessarily identify them as embodied persons. The second of these two necessities would be conditional, but the first would be unconditional, or absolute. It is, of course, only too easy to mistake a conditional necessity for an absolute one, and so to exaggerate the rigidity of the framework which is supposed to underlie all possible developments of language.

So the first point is that, although systematic critical philosophy does not obliterate the line dividing philosophy from science, it does blur it. The second point which ought to be added is that, when philosophy is assimilated to science, it is mechanized and made a matter of skill. Any method which is consciously adopted and exclusively followed is likely to produce this effect, and this is one of the reasons why Wittgenstein hated professional philosophy. But perhaps the danger is greatest when the method approximates to scientific method. For in that case it is especially easy to produce results which are philosophically trivial, however interesting they may be from a psychological or anthropological point of view.

What is the remedy? If it is true that reliance on any method is apt to produce this effect, the remedy cannot merely be to find another method. If it is true that Wittgenstein's later philosophy involved implicit generalizations, because it could not help involving them, the remedy cannot be to philosophize in the completely unsystematic way in which he claimed to be philosophizing in his later period. Certainly he avoided triviality, and possibly he avoided it more conspicuously and more consistently than any other philosopher. But he avoided it by genius, and not by relying on his own later method. In philosophy a method cannot be a recipe.

Part One
Wittgenstein's Early Philosophy

1 The Beginnings

Wittgenstein's philosophy belongs to two different periods
in his life, the first of which began in 1912, when he met
Russell in Cambridge. The work which he started soon
afterwards leads up to the *Tractatus*, which first appeared
in German in 1921, and in English in 1922.[1] After its publication he put aside philosophy. The second period began
in the late 1920s, when he resumed philosophy, and it con-
tinued until his death in 1951. In this period there was a
change not only in the character of his thought, but also in
his attitude to publication. After the *Tractatus* he only
released one other piece of philosophical work in his life,
and that was a short article which appeared in 1929.[2] His
other great work, *Philosophical Investigations*, was published posthumously in 1953. This withdrawal had an un-
nerving effect. A philosopher who was known to be one of
the greatest, if not the greatest alive, had changed his mind,
but the only people who had any direct knowledge of the
change were the privileged few who had heard him lecture
or had had discussions with him.

His work in both periods, like the work of almost every
other linguistic philosopher, is part of the second wave of
critical philosophy. But in his case there is, underneath this
general link with the past, another more specific one. He
took much of the framework of the *Tractatus* from Kant
through Schopenhauer, whom he had read and admired,
and, though he modified this framework in his second

1. It appeared in *Annalen der Naturphilosophie* in 1921. See Biographical Note p. 185.
2. 'Some Remarks on Logical Form' which appeared in Supplementary Vol. IX of the *Proceedings of the Aristotelian Society*.

period, he never destroyed it.

His early philosophy starts at a point which at first sight seems to have no connection with the Kantian framework. It starts as an investigation of the foundations of logic. For he discovered that Russell could not give an adequate explanation of logical necessity, and he believed that the only way to get one would be to go back to the very beginnings of logic, and examine its source in the essential nature of propositions. At first sight, this enterprise does not look particularly Kantian. It might lead to some kind of critique of language, but that would only give it a very general connection with the critical philosophy of Kant. How is it connected with the specifically Kantian character of the system of the *Tractatus*?

This question may be answered in summary form, and the details left to be filled in later. The task which Kant set himself was the demarcation of the limits of thought, and the parallel task which Wittgenstein set himself was the demarcation of the limits of language. Wittgenstein's task may seem to have nothing to do with an investigation of the foundations of logic. But he saw a close connection between the two undertakings because he thought that logic covers everything that is necessarily true, and so can be said in advance of experience; or, to put this in the old terminology, everything that is *a priori*. It is, for example, a contingent fact that the moon is smaller than the earth, and experience was needed to establish it: but it is an *a priori* or necessary truth that it either is or is not smaller than the earth, and that could have been said in advance. Now the limits of language, like the limits of thought were supposed to be necessary limits. So, given Wittgenstein's broad conception of logic, it would be logic that plots them. In this way his investigation of the foundations of logic came to include an inquiry into the limits of language.

The main lines of the system of the *Tractatus*, which give it its specific resemblances to Kant's *Critique of Pure*

Reason, all flow from this point. The limits of thought and the limits of language do not merely happen to lie where they do lie: their location is necessarily determined. So just as Kant maintained that thought necessarily ceases in the rarefied atmosphere beyond the boundary which he plotted, so too Wittgenstein maintained that language necessarily ceases at his line of demarcation, and that beyond it there can only be silence. Kant's boundary enclosed factual knowledge, and Wittgenstein's enclosed factual discourse. In each case the withdrawal from speculative metaphysics left religion and morality in an exposed position. Wittgenstein's solution to this problem, though not the same as Kant's, was very like it; he placed the truths of religion and morality not outside factual discourse, but in some mysterious way inside it without being part of it.

There are, however, several large differences between the two systems. One has already been mentioned: Wittgenstein's critique is an indirect critique of thought through the intermediary of language. Another, less obvious difference is that, although both Kant and Wittgenstein believed that philosophical propositions belong to the realm of necessity, they took very different views not only of philosophical truth but also of necessary truth.

Wittgenstein maintained that all necessity is logical necessity, and that the necessary truths of logic are all empty tautologies. The second of these two theses is his solution to the problem which, according to him, lay unresolved beneath Russell's great development of logic. The two theses, taken together, amount to a denial that there are any necessary truths about matters of substance; *i.e.* in the technical terminology, a denial that there are any synthetic *a priori* truths. Here, then, are some conspicuous differences between Kant's system and the system of the *Tractatus*. For Kant did not develop a comprehensive theory of logic, found tautologies uninteresting and, most important of all, maintained that there are certain substantial necessary truths which hold within the bounds of possible experience. For instance, according to him, the statement that every event has a cause is a necessary truth of this kind. This example, which was mentioned earlier, is perhaps the most important one. But he also claimed to have established other substantial necessary truths, and his view was that together they form the framework of the system of factual knowledge.

If Kant and Wittgenstein agreed that philosophical truths are necessary truths, but disagreed about the nature of necessary truths, there must be consequential differences between their views about philosophical arguments and about the kind of result which they may be expected to establish. What exactly are these consequential differences? A brief answer cannot altogether avoid obscurity, because part of Wittgenstein's early view of the nature of philosophy is difficult to understand. But it is worth while to try to establish a general comparison between the two philosophers' views about their subject, even if it inevitably leaves some points in darkness for the time being.

Kant's view was that the philosopher's task is to establish that the substantial necessary truths, which form the framework of the system of factual knowledge, really do hold within that system, and do not hold outside it. Part of Wittgenstein's early view was that philosophers ought to analyse the meanings of various kinds of statement in order to clarify them. This part of his early view of the nature of philosophy is neither difficult to understand, nor original. Moore and Russell had already developed it, and the kind of result that it produces was familiar. Given that a word has a certain meaning, philosophical analysis can tell us exactly what will necessarily be the case if a statement containing that word happens to be true. Here the necessity will be tautological, or at least definitional, so the analysis will take the form of a statement which has no factual content, and is in that sense empty. For example, the analysis of the phrase 'material object' will take the form, 'If anything is a material object, then the following requirements will necessarily be met ...', and this will be an empty tautology. But that does not mean that the discovery and formulation of such analyses is a simple matter. They are not, as this example would demonstrate if it were worked out.

The more difficult side of Wittgenstein's early view of philosophy, which is the side which should be compared with Kant's view, begins to emerge when we note that the foregoing example is an example of a conditional necessity: given that a word has a certain meaning, something is necessarily true, but, if it has that meaning, the fact that it has it will only be a contingent fact. But philosophical arguments will have to take a different form when they try to establish absolute necessities. Now according to Wittgenstein, the necessity that the limits of language should lie where they do lie is an absolute necessity. So he tried to establish this absolute necessity by deducing it not from some contingent feature of language, but from the essential nature of language. He argued in a way that will be described in detail later that the essential nature of language can be discerned in any actual language; that it follows from this essential nature that any actual language can be analysed into a language of elementary propositions; and that these elementary propositions serve as a point of origin, from which the philosopher, using a logical formula, can calculate the limits of any possible language.

The details of this argument need not concern us for the moment. The important thing is to see the kind of thing that Wittgenstein was trying to do. He was working inside the structure of actual language, and he was trying to establish the limits of any possible language. It is as if a creature living inside the skin of an opaque bubble plotted its centre, and then used some hydraulic formula to calculate the maximum expansion of any possible bubble.

The difficult thing is to understand the status of Wittgenstein's conclusion, and of the argument which was supposed to establish it. The suggestion that the conclusion of the argument, or indeed any of its steps, is absolutely necessary, raises a problem to which his solution is obscure. Certainly this part of his early view of the nature of philosophy is much the more important part. It puts the *Tractatus* in the great tradition of western philosophy, and all the beauty and majesty of the book come from this source. But it is no good pretending that this side of his philosophy is clear.

The problem raised by the argument is that he treats every step in it, including its conclusion, as absolutely necessary, without apparently treating them as empty tautologies. This problem began to appear when we asked how he thought that the essential nature of language could be apprehended. Presumably he did not intend his account of it to be taken as an empty definition. But if the necessary truths of this part of philosophy are substantial, how are they apprehended? This is only the beginning of the problem. The deeper difficulty is that, however they are apprehended, they seem to be substantial necessary truths, and yet, according to him, there are no such necessary truths. The difficulty becomes more conspicuous when he takes a further step, and tries to deduce the structure of reality from the lattice of elementary propositions which he believed to be the basic structure of all languages. How is this ontological conclusion meant to be taken? It can hardly be meant as an empty tautology about reality in so far as it can be caught in the network of a language which satisfies his preferred definition. So is it supposed to be a substantial necessary truth about reality in so far as it can be caught in the network of any language? Or is it offered as a substantial necessary truth about reality without that qualification?

Wittgenstein does not appear to have chosen between the last two interpretations, and this may be because he did not see any real difference between them. However, the difficulty still remains. Kant could use substantial necessary truths to construct the framework of his system, but Wittgenstein's theory of necessity left him in no position to follow Kant on this point.

It is not clear how he proposed to remove the apparent inconsistency. In fact, the criticisms of the *Tractatus* which he makes in *Philosophical Investigations* suggest that he had no effective way of removing it. However, there is a line of thought which may have once seemed to him to lead to a solution. He says again and again in the *Tractatus* that philosophical propositions do not lie within the limits of language. But what kind of a solution would lie in that direction? According to him, what lies beyond the limits of language cannot be asserted in language, but can only be shown. But what would be the status of something that can only be shown? Would it be a necessary truth, and, if so, what sort of necessary truth would it be? This avenue will now be explored, but no clear result is to be expected.

The first thing to be noted is that Wittgenstein's ontological conclusion is recondite. His view about the structure of reality was that it is composed of simple objects, which he calls 'objects' leaving the qualification to be understood, and that this structure is precisely mirrored in the structure of elementary propositions. A detailed exposition of this view is not required at the moment, because the point that needs to be made about it is a general one : we would not expect to find in ordinary factual discourse either the philosophical proposition in which the ontological thesis is expressed or any mention of things of the type which it mentions. So if this proposition describes the framework of factual discourse, that framework is remote and unfamiliar to us. There is here a sharp contrast with the way in which Kant sets up the framework of his system of factual knowledge. The philosophical propositions which he uses for this purpose are, or at least most of them are, not at all recondite, and in the course of an ordinary factual inquiry there might well be mention of the kind of thing which they mention. For example, the proposition 'Every event has a cause' was not first formulated by philosophers, and the application of the concept of cause to particular cases is something very familiar. So Kant's framework stands out on the surface.

A concealed framework needs a penetrating investigation to establish its existence. This certainly explains one feature of Wittgenstein's early philosophy, its depth. But it does not explain what he meant when he said that philosophical propositions do not lie within the limits of language. For elementary propositions do lie within the limits of language, and yet they have precisely this recondite character.

At this point it is important to remember that, when Wittgenstein speaks of the limits of language in the *Tractatus*, he means the limits of factual discourse. Therefore his view about philosophical propositions is that at least they are neither factual nor contingent. But to what positive category do they belong? Is this negative characterization of them the only possible one? If so, his view about the nature of the propositions which belong to this part of his philosophy will suffer from the obscurity of excessive generality, and no solution to the present problem will have been reached. For, of course, tautologies too are neither factual nor contingent, and the problem at the moment is to establish a more specific categorization of his theory of language and his theory of reality. The two theories, which are really one, can hardly be meant to be tautological. So they must have some further characteristic which differentiates them. Yet that characteristic cannot be substantial necessary truth, if Wittgenstein is to be consistent.

Now he certainly offered a further specification of the theory of language and the ontology of the *Tractatus*, and he attached great importance to his further specification of them. He claimed that his theories were good metaphysical theories. Admittedly, they made the general metaphysical mistake of trying to say what can only be shown. But he claimed that what they try to say is something valid. So the thesis that there must be objects would be a good metaphysical thesis. It is true that the concept of an object is a formal concept, and so we ought not to say that there are objects, because that makes their existence sound contingent, as if we were saying that there are coelocanths. The correct way to present the existence of objects would be to use propositions in which their names occur. Then their existence could be seen through these propositions, but it would not be asserted by them, and could not properly be asserted by any proposition which contained the word 'object'. It is something that can be shown but not said. Similarly, the logical relation between the propositions 'p' and 'not-p' cannot properly be asserted by any third proposition. It can be seen in the form of the two propositions themselves, or it can be demonstrated by combining them in the tautology 'p or not-p'. But a tautology is not a factual proposition and it makes no assertion. So here is another thing that can be shown but not said.

But it is not clear that this further specification of the theory of language and the ontology of the *Tractatus* leads to any solution of the present problem. The difficulty is that Wittgenstein's ontological conclusion is not merely that there are objects, but that there must be objects. It is, therefore, not enough to apologize for using the formal concept of an object as if it were an ordinary concept. An explanation of the force of the word 'must' is also required. Does it or does it not express a substantial necessary truth? If this question is not unaskable, the answer would seem to be that it does express a substantial necessary truth. The argument for this answer has already been given: surely there is a difference between the necessary truth of a tautology and the necessary truth of the theory which is presupposed by the system of factual discourse. But what did Wittgenstein take the difference to be? In default of a clear answer from him, it is natural to conclude that in the end his system is like Kant's, although on the way to this destination it exhibits many differences, one of which is incompatible with the journey.

This can hardly be a firm conclusion without a more detailed examination of Wittgenstein's early philosophy. But before that is undertaken, there is one last general remark which ought to be made. However much light may be thrown on his early system by the comparison and contrast with Kant's system, it would be a mistake to suppose that he merely revived Kant's themes in a new key with certain variations. His philosophy began as an investigation of the foundations of logic, and his point of departure was the great work already done on logic by Frege and by Russell, and Russell's teaching in Cambridge. Of course, it might still have been the case that, when he came to the question, what philosophy is, he derived his answer, that it is a critique of language, directly from Kant and Schopenhauer, with the familiar modulation from thought to language. But in fact this is not what happened. For when he arrived in Cambridge in 1912, philosophy had already begun to move into this new critical phase, largely under the influence of Russell and Moore. Wittgenstein's early philosophy must be seen for what it is, a complex work of genius, in which ideas of many different kinds are combined, and questions which seem to be almost out of earshot of one another find connected answers.

2   The Limits of Language

In his Preface to the *Tractatus* Wittgenstein says that the aim of the book is to plot the limits of language. But before he says this he says that the book deals with the problems of philosophy. He explains the connection between the two tasks by saying that the reason why the problems of philosophy are posed is that the logic of our language is misunderstood. He acknowledges his debt to Frege and Russell, but he does not attempt to explain how questions in the theory of logic are connected with either of the two tasks which he has just mentioned. He ends the Preface by making two claims for his book: it lays down the general lines of a final solution to the problems of philosophy, and it shows how little is achieved when those problems are solved.

Each of these assertions carries a heavy load of meaning. The second claim alludes to the greater importance of religion and morality. When he speaks of the limits of language, he means the limits of factual language, and the philosophical problems which he has in mind are posed, as they nearly always are posed, in terms which do not clearly distinguish them from factual problems. His first claim is that these philosophical problems are solved by a critique of language which fixes the limits of factual discourse. The curtailment of factual discourse leaves religion and morality in a position which he describes towards the end of the book. The Preface suggests that philosophy is finished, but it must be observed that, whatever has happened to the body of traditional philosophy, its spirit has certainly migrated into Wittgenstein's critique of language. The question, what the status of this critique is, is not raised in the Preface, and it is not until the end of the book that we are told that it too tries to say in a factual way things which cannot be said in a factual way, and so after its other work has been done it must turn round and eliminate itself.

The text of the *Tractatus* is formidably difficult. Part of the difficulty is that the intricate construction of the book makes it hard to find a clear point of entry into it. Certainly the way in is not through its opening sentences. Fortunately, we possess some of the notebooks in which Wittgenstein worked out the ideas which later went into the *Tractatus*.[1] The *Tractatus* is brief, enigmatic, and therefore apparently confident, but when the same topics are discussed in the *Notebooks*, the treatment is more extended, and brings in conflicting arguments, and it is sometimes tormented by doubts. So when a comparison between the two books is possible, it throws a lot of light on the *Tractatus*. Now the *Notebooks* begin as an inquiry into the foundations of logic, and that point of entry into the system of the *Tractatus* was used in the summary account of it which has already been given. Here the system will be entered at a different point, which is suggested by what Wittgenstein says in his Preface. The first question that will be asked is the question how the task of plotting the limits of factual discourse is to be carried out.

The task is a difficult one, because there is no Archimedian point outside all factual discourse on which the philosopher can take his stand and still speak in factual terms. 'All' really does mean 'all'. So he needs some way of working from inside factual discourse. The method used by Wittgenstein has already been described in a general way. He divided the task into two stages. First, he worked back from the skin of the bubble of ordinary factual discourse to its notional centre, elementary propositions. Then using a

1. *Notebooks 1914–1916*, edited by G. H. von Wright and G. E. M. Anscombe, with an English translation by G. E. M. Anscombe: Blackwell, 1961. See Bibliography, p. 187.

logical formula he worked outwards again to the limit of expansion of the bubble. These two stages now need to be described in detail.

But first something must be said about the general feel of the task, and the kind of results which might be expected if it were successfully carried out. Anyone who undertakes it will naturally tell himself that, as Wittgenstein puts it in his Preface, on the other side of the limit lies nonsense. But this needs to be qualified in more ways than one. For as he points out later in the *Tractatus*, there is no other side to the limit, and so the task of plotting it is more like calculating the curvature of space itself. If the senses of factual propositions are points in logical space, nonsense is nowhere.

There is also another qualification that is needed. If the limits of sense are the limits of factual discourse, all nonfactual discourse will be nonsense. So it looks as if anyone who sees the task of demarcation in this way will be a positivist of the destructive type. However, there are two other possibilities. He might stretch the term 'factual discourse' to cover more than it usually covers, and in that case the space of factual discourse would acquire a more sinuous curve which would allow for the gravitational pull of whatever it is that is happening in the less scientific fields of thought. Or he might draw some subtle distinction between good and bad nonsense. Wittgenstein was completely opposed to the first of these two alternatives, but he developed the second in the way that has already been sketched. By refusing to locate the truths of religion and morality within factual discourse, he was not rejecting them, but trying to preserve them. They are non-sense because they lack factual sense. But to make this point about them is not to condemn them as unintelligible. It is to take the first step towards understanding them.

The first part of Wittgenstein's task of demarcation was to work back from ordinary factual propositions to the elementary propositions which, according to him, lie at its centre. But when he does this in the *Tractatus*, it is difficult to see exactly how he does it. It is, of course, evident that he takes over the kind of analysis that was practised by Russell and Moore, and builds a theory around it. But that is a very inadequate description of his procedure, because his theory is not a general account of the current practice of logical analysis, but an original and entirely general theory of factual meaning. This theory is based on two axioms, which for the moment will merely be labelled X and Y, because it would overburden the exposition to give their content immediately. The point to be borne in mind is that, according to Wittgenstein, X and Y, taken together, give the essence of language, and the question which was asked earlier, how this essence is apprehended, becomes the question, how X and Y are established.

First, it is necessary to describe Wittgenstein's general line of thought. His starting point was ordinary factual discourse. But like Russell he did not leave ordinary factual propositions in the form in which they are current in everyday life, or even in science. He believed that language disguises thought, and that the real forms of our thoughts would become apparent only when the language in which they are expressed had been analysed and broken down into its ultimate components, which according to him, are elementary propositions. His idea was that the assertion of an ordinary factual proposition is a gross move, which contains within itself a large number of minute moves. For example, merely to assert that the watch is lying on the table is to assert by implication many other propositions, which in this case might be propositions about the mechanism inside the watch. But this would only be the first generation of implications. For these propositions themselves would imply others, which would imply others, and so on, until we reached the ultimate components of the original proposition, at which point the analysis would be complete. Naturally, Wittgenstein was not recommending that the assertion of each of these implied propositions should be a separate move in everyday life. The grossness of ordinary factual propositions is a blessing. His point was that an exact account of what they mean could be given only if they were analysed into their ultimate compónents, elementary propositions.

It is mystifying to introduce elementary propositions without immediately explaining what they are. But there is a real difficulty here. Wittgenstein did not claim to be able to give any examples of elementary propositions, because he thought that neither he nor any other philosopher had yet got down to the ultimate components of factual propositions. Now the point that must be borne in mind is that, even if logical analysis had penetrated to that level, so that he could have given examples of elementary propositions, he would still have needed his general theory of meaning. For he would not have been content with demonstrating that the complete analyses of certain factual propositions happen to contain elementary propositions: he had to prove that the complete analyses of all factual propositions are necessarily composed entirely of elementary propositions. This conclusion could not be established inductively by using logical analysis on a few chosen cases: it had to be deduced from a general theory of meaning. Nevertheless, some examples of elementary propositions would have been a help. In default of examples we have to rely entirely on Wittgenstein's specification of elementary propositions. He specifies them as a class of factual propositions which are logically independent of one another: the truth or falsity of one elementary proposition never implies the truth or falsity of any other elementary proposition.

So the first part of his task was to prove, as a deduction from his theory of meaning, that all factual propositions are analysable without remainder into minute factual pro-

positions which are logically independent of one another
There are three questions about this enterprise which have
to be answered. What was his theory of meaning? How
was it established? And how did the deduction proceed?

Any theory presupposes a question to which it is an
answer. Wittgenstein's theory of meaning was an answer to
the question, how factual propositions get their senses. Now
it must not be forgotten that this question arose in Wittgenstein's mind out of another question, the question what
logical necessity is. He believed that logical necessity could
be explained only if it were traced back to its source in the
essential nature of propositions. So when he asked how
factual propositions get their senses, he was looking for an
answer which would be rich in consequences.

His answer was a theory of meaning based on axioms X
and Y, which must now be given. X says that every factual
proposition has a precise sense: Y says that the way in
which every factual proposition gets this sense is pictorial.
A rough description of the relationship between these two
axioms would be that X analyses the problem and Y solves
it. To have a sense is to have a precise sense, and a factual
proposition gets its precise sense only because its words represent things, just as a diagram says something only if its
parts represent things.

But do things that are represented have to exist in order
to be represented? There is a dilemma here. For if they do
not have to exist, it is not clear how they get represented:
and if they do have to exist, Y is open to the obvious objection that a factual proposition might well have a sense even
if it contained a word which happened to represent something which did not exist. This can happen, just as it can
happen that a certain part of a diagram represents something that does not exist, perhaps an invention. However,
what can be said in such cases is that, if the whole diagram
is going to be intelligible, that particular part of it must be
divisible into elements which represent things that do exist.

For example, the first man to think of a watch spring could produce a diagram of it by drawing a wheel and an axle and a coil, and by showing the tension, and these types of things would already exist. This suggests a reformulation of Y which escapes the dilemma: a factual proposition gets its precise sense only because its words either themselves represent existing things or are analysable into other words which represent existing things. For the symbolization of facts is based on the representation of things by words, and a word cannot represent a thing unless it is correlated with it, and correlation with non-existent things is impossible. The sort of correlation which Wittgenstein had in mind is the correlation of a name with the thing named.

But what is the point of insisting, as X does, that the senses of all factual propositions must be precise? The sense of a proposition is a function of its implications: it depends on what is necessarily the case if the proposition is true. So to say that a proposition must have a precise sense is to say that it must be possible to draw a sharp line around everything that is necessarily the case if it is true. Within this enclosure all its implications would stand up to be counted. Together they would make a definite claim on reality, which would either satisfy the claim, in which case the proposition would be true, or not satisfy it, in which case the proposition would be false. There is no third possibility. So X states a requirement which any factual proposition must meet: what is required of it is that its analysis should not terminate until it is clear exactly how the law of excluded middle applies to it.

When X is developed in this way, it becomes clear that it is not a purely neutral reformulation of the problem, how factual propositions get their senses, but a substantial contribution towards its solution. Yet X is supposed to be a necessary truth. So here is one point at which Wittgenstein confronted the difficult question, how substantial necessary truths can be established—the second of the three questions asked at the beginning of this discussion. Even if he were able to answer this question, there would still be the difficulty that there does not seem to be any place for substantial necessary truths in his system. But perhaps enough has been said about these difficulties, and all that we need to do now is to bring out the point of substance which X contains. It is a point of substance, and not a tautology that every proposition has a precise sense. For it would be possible, without denying the law of excluded middle, to deny that it can be applied to every factual proposition in the way that X applies it. Some factual propositions might be inherently vague. Wittgenstein himself makes this point against X in *Philosophical Investigations*, and raises the interesting general question, whether logic idealizes the structure of language and, if so, to what extent.

Y too is a substantial thesis about factual propositions, and not a tautology. But before demonstrating this point, it would be as well to answer the third question on the list, by putting X and Y together, in order to show how Wittgenstein deduced from them the conclusion that the complete analyses of all factual propositions are necessarily composed entirely of elementary propositions.

His deduction is complicated by the fact that it requires an auxiliary assumption, Z. Z is the thesis that, whenever two propositions are logically related to one another, there will be within one of the two, or within both, some logical complexity which analysis could reveal. For example, the propositions 'p' and 'not-p' are logically incompatible with one another, and so at least one of the two must contain some logical complexity which would explain the incompatibility. In this case, however difficult it may be to give a general account of logical necessity, it is evident that 'not-p' is the culprit. Now from Wittgenstein's original specification of elementary propositions it follows that 'p' and 'not-p' cannot both be elementary, because there is that logical relationship between them, and it is plain that, even if 'p' happens to be elementary, this cannot be the case with 'not-p'.

The plot thickens when Z is applied to propositions whose logical relationships are based on words which, unlike the word 'not', purport to represent things. For though Z clearly works in some cases of this kind, in others it breaks down, or at least appears to break down. It works with the incompatible pair 'This creature is a mammal' and 'This creature is a fish', and perhaps even with the incompatible pair 'This town is Dartmouth' and 'This town is Exmouth'. For the word at the end of each of these four propositions is logically complex, or, to put the same point in what Carnap called 'the material mode of speech',[2] the thing which each of these words purports to represent is logically complex: and at least in the case of the first pair logical analysis could bring the complexity to the surface by substituting definitions for the final words. But Z seems to break down on the incompatible pair. 'This thing is blue' and 'This thing is yellow'. For what definitions of the two colour-words would explain this logical relationship? Of course, a proponent of Z is not forced to admit that it breaks down at this point, because he can still maintain that there must be hidden definitions of the two colour-words, and that the discovery of their definitions would be a triumph of logical analysis which would vindicate Z in this kind of case as well as in the easier kind of case.

Whatever the fate of Z, it is at least clear that it contains a point of substance, because it can be denied without self-contradiction and so cannot be tautological. For it is not self-contradictory to suggest that, though the incompatibility between the two colour-words is logical, it does not depend on their internal complexity, because, though colour-words form a system, their systematic connections with one another cannot be packed into definitions of the

2. R. Carnap: *The Logical Syntax of Language*, Routledge & Kegan Paul, London, 1937, pp. 237 ff and 286 ff.

individual words. As a matter of fact, Wittgenstein abandoned Z before X and Y, and when he abandoned it, he moved off in this direction. But the details of his retractation can wait till later.

What led him to accept Z at the time when he compiled the *Tractatus*? A possible answer is that the kind of logical pluralism which Z expresses is very satisfying, because it frames things separately and presents them for contemplation one by one. It is also a theory which is particularly well adapted to the practice of logical analysis, because it suggests that piecemeal work may be rewarded by definite progress. However, though these two points may explain why Russell accepted logical pluralism, they do not explain Wittgenstein's acceptance of it so well. For Wittgenstein always had a strong bent towards holism, or monism, as the theory which is opposed to pluralism is sometimes called. In his case part of the explanation lies in the historical accident of his early association with Russell. But there is also a powerful theoretical reason behind his acceptance of Z. In his hands Z led, via the deduction which will now be set out, to his theory of elementary propositions, and this theory is a version of logical atomism which yields a uniform explanation of all necessary truths except the philosophical propositions which belong to the system of the *Tractatus*. This advantage of logical pluralism will be explained later. Logical atomism is, as its name suggests, the extreme development of logical pluralism: analysis can go no further.

We are now in a position to set out Wittgenstein's deduction of the thesis that the complete analyses of all factual propositions are necessarily composed entirely of elementary propositions. His argument takes the form of a *reductio ad absurdum*. The hypothesis which has to be proved absurd is, of course, the denial of his own conclusion: he has to prove the absurdity of the suggestion that the complete analysis of a factual proposition might contain some non-elementary propositions.

His original specification of elementary propositions distinguished them as a class of factual propositions which are logically independent of one another. All other factual propositions, which are non-elementary, do have logical relations with one another. Now it follows from Z that non-elementary propositions, since they are logically related to one another, must have some internal complexity, which would be revealed by logical analysis. Therefore, if a non-elementary proposition occurred in the complete analysis of a factual proposition, it would contain a complex word which purported to represent a complex thing. At this point Y must be brought into the argument. Y says that a factual proposition gets its sense only because its words either represent existing things or are analysable into other words which represent existing things. But the second alternative is ruled out in this case, because the hypothesis is that the analysis in which the complex word occurs is already complete. Therefore, on this hypothesis, the original factual proposition will have a sense only if that word really does represent an existing complex thing.

So far, no absurdity has been found in the hypothesis. But the trouble begins to emerge when Wittgenstein points out that, if the complex thing exists, it follows logically that a further proposition, which analyses its complexity and asserts its existence, will be true: for example, it will be true that there is a town at the mouth of the river Dart. So if the original factual proposition has a sense, it follows logically that this further proposition, which lies beyond the termination of its analysis, will be true. Moreover, if the original factual proposition is true, it must have a sense, and so, if it is true, it follows logically that the further proposition beyond the termination of its own analysis will be true.

But what is absurd about this? Nothing, until we bring in X. For according to X the sense of a proposition includes everything which is necessarily the case if it is true, and from this it follows that the further proposition must be included in the sense of the original proposition. But this really is absurd, because it contradicts the hypothesis that the analysis of the original proposition had terminated before the further proposition had been reached. Furthermore, suppose that, guided by X, we did include the further proposition in the analysis of the original proposition, just as we might include the details of anything complex, which was represented by a picture, in the message conveyed by the whole picture. Then exactly the same argument could be used again at the next stage, and it would push the limit of analysis one notch further out. But X requires that the sense of a factual proposition should be precise, and so that there should be an end to this process of aggrandizement. A country, whose frontier was always a little further out than at any moment it was deemed to be, would not really have a frontier, and so would not be a territorial unit at all. Similarly, the aggrandizement of the sense of a proposition must come to a halt. There must be a definite limit to what is being asserted, and so there must be a definite limit to the view into reality which is presented by a picture or a factual proposition. Both may have a very fine grain, but in each case there must be a definite limit to the fineness of the grain.

This is an abstract argument, based on a general theory of meaning, and Wittgenstein did not claim to be able to produce any examples of complete analyses which might reinforce its conclusion, or even illustrate it. He merely specified elementary propositions as a class of logically independent factual propositions, and he left the precise nature of their elements, which he called 'names', shrouded in mystery. Now these names were pure names, which, unlike the name 'Dartmouth', had no concealed factual content. So their meanings could only be the simple objects, or, as he puts it, leaving the qualification to be understood, the 'objects', which they represented. But what sort of thing is an object?

This question, to which there is no answer in the *Tractatus*, is rather like a question about the first years of Hamlet's life. Wittgenstein's theory of meaning lays down certain general requirements for elementary propositions, and the full characterization of them may be anything that satisfies these requirements. It is, therefore, no good expecting to find an answer to the question whether the objects of the *Tractatus* are material particles or the sense-data of human observers. As a matter of fact, he uses examples of both these kinds, but without committing himself to either, because, of course, his theory of factual meaning was entirely general, and he did not want its application to be restricted by irrelevant arguments drawn from the theory of knowledge. His elementary propositions are mysterious, and that is a fact about the *Tractatus* which has to be accepted.

It is, incidentally, a fact which explains the kind of influence exerted by the *Tractatus* between the two wars. Although the method of analysis which it described was not new, the systematic theory which he built around it, and the great claims which he made for it increased the impetus of the linguistic movement in philosophy: but the theory helped to produce this result only in an indirect way, because, though it was new, it was not the sort of thing that could be used, and the description of elementary propositions gave more inspiration than guidance, like the pictures which are sometimes found inset in old maps.

Elementary propositions lie at the centre of the system of factual discourse, and constitute its inner limit. The first stage in Wittgenstein's demarcation of the system was to fix this inner limit, because it was the point of origin from which he was to work outwards and calculate its outer limit, the maximum expansion of the bubble. The second stage, the calculation of the outer limit, is much easier to describe. This is partly because it is less complicated, and partly because his method of calculating the outer limit is really the reverse operation of his method of fixing the point of origin. For if the complete analyses of all factual propositions are necessarily composed entirely of elementary propositions, it follows that all factual propositions can be constructed entirely out of elementary propositions. The process of synthesis is simply the process of analysis in reverse.

But although this is true, it leaves many details to be filled in. For too little has been said about the process of analysis, and so it is not sufficiently informative to say that it was simply put into reverse. Also not enough has been said about Y, and a detailed account of the method of constructing factual propositions would fill this gap too.

3 Pictures and Logic

Wittgenstein's theory of factual propositions depends on a single fundamental idea, the idea of exclusion. A factual proposition always excludes, or shuts out a certain possibility. In the simplest case the proposition 'p' asserts the possibility *not-p* out of existence, or rather, since speech does not have magical powers, it claims that it does not exist, and to do this is to show it the door. Moreover, that is all that it does. For to exclude the possibility *not-p* is to say 'not-not-p', and 'not-not-p' is logically equivalent to 'p'. It is a logical necessity that there be no third possibility between *p* and *not-p*, as it were *half-p*, and this logical necessity is expressed in the law of excluded middle.

It is, of course, essential to distinguish the exclusion of *half-p*, which is logically necessary, from the exclusion of *not-p*, which is done by the factual proposition 'p'. For what is excluded by a logical truth could not be the case, whereas what is excluded by a factual proposition might be the case, and all that the factual proposition does is to claim that it contingently is not the case. So perhaps it would be better to mark this difference by saying that the proposition 'p' shuts out the possibility *not-p*, rather than that it excludes it.

Now it must be remembered that Wittgenstein had to work out a theory of factual propositions which would yield an adequate explanation of logical necessity. So he had to discover a connection between the shutting out which is done by factual propositions and the excluding which is done by logical propositions. The connection which he found was that what is shut out by a factual proposition is something, whereas what is excluded by a logical proposition is nothing.

But taken out of its context this is only an obscure epigram, and Wittgenstein's theory needs to be built up visibly around it. So let us look next at a more complicated case. Suppose that 'p' is a non-elementary proposition, and that its analysis is 'q and r' (this analysis need not be complete, and so 'q' and 'r' may be non-elementary too). Then what 'p' shuts out is the possibility *either not-q or not-r or both*. A moment's reflection shows that 'p' is really shutting out three separate compound possibilities: the first is the possibility *not-q and r*, the second is the possibility *q and not-r* and the third is the possibility *both not-q and not-r*. Moreover, since the relevant compound possibilities are all constructed out of the two basic possibilities *q* and *r*, there is only one more which can be constructed, *viz. q and r*. Because this is the only remaining possibility, the proposition 'q and r' is asserting its existence by shutting out the other three possibilities. Or, to put the same point in the other way, the proposition 'not (either not-q or not-r or both)' is logically equivalent to the proposition 'q and r', and so logically equivalent to the original proposition 'p', of which 'q and r' is the analysis. Thus the entire sense of 'p' is given by saying which of the four compound possibilities it shuts out.

Wittgenstein's next step is to generalize this result. According to him, the entire sense of every factual proposition is given by constructing the complete list of relevant possibilities in the way in which it was constructed in the last example, and by saying which of these possibilities the proposition shuts out. Now the method of construction used in that example was first to take the proposition 'p' and analyse it into 'q and r'; then to take 'q' and 'r' and add their negations 'not-q' and 'not-r'; and then finally to take the four corresponding possibilities, *q, r, not-q*, and *not-r*, and combine them to form the four relevant compound possibilities, *q and r, q and not-r, not-q and r*, and *not-q and not-r*. This method of construction will always yield 2^n relevant possibilities, where n is the number of propositions in the analysis at the original proposition. Then, according to Wittgenstein, the entire sense of any factual proposition is given by saying which of the 2^n possibilities it shuts out. To put the same point in another way, the truth or falsity of any factual proposition depends solely on the truth or falsity of the propositions in its analysis: or, to put this in the usual technical terminology, any factual proposition is a truth-function of the propositions in its analysis. This controversial thesis is called 'the thesis of extensionality'.

One more step is needed to complete Wittgenstein's task. If the limit of language is to include all factual propositions, the thesis of extensionality must be applied to elementary propositions. For if he applied it to non-elementary propositions, he would leave out some of the possible truth-functions, because the base to which it was applied would be incompletely analysed: just as an architect who worked with prefabricated units would have fewer possibilities open to him than one who worked with bricks. So his final conclusion is that all factual propositions are truth-functions of elementary propositions.

Although this theory of factual discourse fixes its outer limit in relation to elementary propositions, it does not fix it absolutely. For there is no answer to the question precisely what type of proposition elementary propositions are, and so there is no exact fix for the point of origin of the whole survey. Wittgenstein was careful not to commit himself to the view that acquaintance with the objects named in elementary propositions would have to be sensory, or to the view that it could not be sensory. Between alternatives such as these his theory of factual propositions is entirely neutral. However, it is not this neutrality which proves that he was not a positivist of the destructive type. For it is clear that he did not include the propositions of religion and morality among factual propositions, and so his neutrality about the point of origin of the system of factual propositions was certainly not intended to allow for the possibility that some of them might be non-empirical. What proves that he was not a positivist is his attitude to the propositions of religion and morality after he has put them outside the factual domain.

The aloofness of this theory of meaning and its detachment from any particular theory of knowledge are conspicuous. What is not so easy to discern is how it came to be so detached. In this case the theory of knowledge which is the opposite number is empiricism, the theory that all factual knowledge is based on sensory experience. Maybe this is too vague to be called a theory, and perhaps it becomes a theory only when the precise nature of the base has been specified. Certainly it becomes an instrument of destruction only if all claims to non-factual knowledge are automatically rejected, as they are by extreme positivists. It becomes a theory of meaning, if it maintains that the sensory material which it specifies forms the base from which the meanings of all factual propositions are constructed. This kind of theory of meaning becomes a weapon in the hands of the extreme positivist because he automatically rejects all non-factual propositions as utter nonsense, and not merely as non-sense.

Now three points have been made about Wittgenstein's theory of factual meaning. It contained nothing which would make it impossible to apply it to an empirical base, as the philosophers of the Vienna Circle[1] applied it: but

1. The Vienna Circle included M. Schlick, F. Waismann and R. Carnap. The *Tractatus* had been studied by the Circle before 1927, when Schlick persuaded Wittgenstein to meet Waismann and Carnap and have philosophical discussions with them. After 1929 Wittgenstein excluded Carnap from these discussions. See R. Carnap: 'Autobiography', in *The Philosophy of Rudolf Carnap*: ed. P. A. Schilpp: now published by The Open Court Publishing Co., La Salle, Illinois. Wittgenstein's discussions with Schlick and Waismann between

this would only be one possible application of it, because it did not include empiricism as part of itself; and, even if it had, it would not have been positivistic. A fourth point, which was made earlier, was that the reason why Wittgenstein kept his theory of meaning detached from empiricism was that he did not want its application to be restricted by irrelevant arguments drawn from the theory of knowledge. But none of these points explains how the detachment came about. This question can be presented in a precise form. For it is really a question about Z. In Russell's hands Z was an axiom of empiricism, taken over from Hume and translated out of the primitive psychological terminology of the eighteenth century into the new logical terminology. But though it is easy to see that Z underwent a much greater change of character in Wittgenstein's hands, it is not so easy to see how this change came about.

A large part of the answer to this question is that Wittgenstein did not share Russell's concern with the way in which the senses of factual proposition are learned. He was concerned with the basic structure of their senses, and it made no difference to him that this structure lay below the level at which learning takes place. This is the point at which he really diverges from Russell. It is comparatively unimportant that Russell's simple particulars are sense-data, whereas the precise nature of Wittgenstein's objects is left unspecified. For if perception were explained in the right way, it might become clear that the senses of factual propositions are not really learned through acquaintance with sense-data; and if sense-data were analysed in the right way, it might become clear that the basic structure of the senses of factual propositions really is exhibited by sense-data. But on the second of these two issues Wittgenstein had not formed an opinion, and he did not need to form one, be-

---

1929 and 1932 are recorded in *Ludwig Wittgenstein und der Wiener Kreis*, ed. B. F. McGuinness, Suhrkamp Verlag, 1967.

cause he took his stand on the requirement that elementary propositions must be logically independent of one another. He was not unduly worried by the fact that neither Russell's sense-datum propositions nor any other type of proposition which anyone had yet suggested, met this requirement. But the really crucial point is that he was not interested in the first issue, because he was not concerned with the way in which the senses of factual propositions are learned.

In spite of this he talks about his objects in a way that suggests that the meanings of his pure names could be learned from them. He also refers to the possibility of acquaintance (*kennen*) with them, and 'acquaintance' is Rússell's word for the cognitive relationship between people and his simple particulars, which are sense-data. This borrowing of the apparatus of empiricism is surprising. The explanation can only be that Wittgenstein did not rule out the possibility of acquaintance with his objects, or even of learning the senses of elementary propositions from them. His theory may be regarded as a speculative projection of the apparatus of empiricism. When he took over the logical ideas on which Russell's theory of analysis was based, he developed them in the darker manner of German Idealism. The *Tractatus* belongs to the same tradition as the work of Freud. It is, of course, neither a psychological treatise nor a philosophical treatise presented in psychological terms. But it offers a speculative theory about something which is usually supposed to take place in the clear light of consciousness, the correlation of words with things, through which factual propositions get their senses. In the case of Wittgenstein's elementary propositions this correlation takes place in total obscurity. If it is something that we do, we do not do it consciously or intentionally.

This is not the only case in which Wittgenstein borrows an idea from the theory of knowledge, and, because he is detached from such issues, is able to transform it and use it in his own way. The process is characteristic of his thought in the *Tractatus*, and more generally of his very unusual kind of originality. Old ideas take root in his mind and begin a new life. In the *Tractatus* the most striking example is his treatment of Solipsism, which he connects with his theory about the limits of language.

The Solipsist's predicament is that, when he denies the existence of everything except himself and the world of his own experiences, he is unable to point to what it is that, according to him, does not exist, because it lies outside his world. So, to use one of Wittgenstein's later analogies, when he points to himself and his own world and claims that they do exist, he is like a man who carefully constructs a clock, and then attaches the dial to the hour-hand so that they both go round together. There is no contrast with anything outside his world. Wittgenstein's predicament, when he sets out to plot the limit of factual discourse, is that he is unable to say that certain named objects exist and that certain others do not exist, because their names are pure names, and the objects themselves would be the meanings of such names. Therefore he draws the limit from the inside, and, if the existence of certain objects could be directly inferred from language, that would not be because their existence was asserted in any propositions, but because it was reflected in the pure names correlated with them. Again there is no contrast, because there is no possibility of going on to name objects which do not exist.

So there is something in the point that the Solipsist is trying to make about what exists. Only certain things exist, but that they exist is something that cannot be said. It can only be shown, and the Solipsist's mistake is to try to express it in a factual proposition, or perhaps in a substantial necessary truth. He himself would probably resist this description of his case. He would object that he can identify the experiences that he means without going outside his world for a contrast: he can identify them as 'the ones that belong to me, to my unique self'. Therefore, he will claim, he has a substantial thesis. But what is this unique self, of whose existence he feels assured? It is neither his body nor his soul nor anything else in his world. It is only the metaphysical subject, which is a kind of focal vanishing point behind the mirror of his language. There is really nothing except the mirror and what the mirror reflects. So the only thing that he can legitimately say is that what is reflected in the mirror is reflected in the mirror. But that is neither a factual thesis nor a substantial necessary truth about what is reflected in the mirror, but a tautology. It means only that whatever objects exist exist. So when Solipsism is worked out, it becomes clear that there is no difference between it and Realism. Moreover, since the unique self is nothing, it would be equally possible to take an impersonal view of the vanishing point behind the mirror of language. Language would then be any language, the metaphysical subject would be the world spirit, and Idealism would lie on the route from Solipsism to Realism. Wittgenstein takes all three of these steps in the *Notebooks*, but in the *Tractatus* he takes only the first, which is also associated with Realism. However, this does not affect his two main points: that all such metaphysical theses are attempts to say things which cannot be said in language but can only be shown, and that Solipsism is a good metaphysical thesis, because there is something in the point that it is trying to make. Many of these ideas came from Schopenhauer, but Wittgenstein's use of them is his own.

Z came from Russell, and X came from Frege. What was the origin of Y, the so-called 'picture theory of propositions'? This was Wittgenstein's own idea, unlike X and Z, which he did not originate, however original his development of them was. Now Y's contribution to the task of demarcating factual language has been described, but the point of substance which Y contains has not yet been isolated, and Wittgenstein's explanation of logical necessity, which depends on Y, still remains to be given.

According to Y, a factual proposition gets its sense only because its words either themselves represent existing things or are analysable into other words which represent existing things. But it has also been pointed out that Wittgenstein maintained that the entire sense of a factual proposition is given by constructing the complete list of relevant possibilities and saying which of them the proposition shuts out. This thesis has been left hanging in the air, as if it might be another axiom or independent assumption in his theory of meaning. But in fact it is not independent, but part of the development of Y.

The simplest way to see this is to start from the fact that the German word 'Bild' means not only 'picture' but also 'model'. Now suppose that someone silently produces a model in order to convey a piece of information; for example, an astronaut makes a clay model of his lost vehicle. In such a case the model may be thought of as something which shuts out of existence the possibility which does not conform to it, just as the proposition 'p' shuts out the possibility *not-p*.

But this does not take the assimilation of propositions and models very far. It only amounts to the platitude that, if a model is used instead of the proposition 'p', it will take over the logical characteristics of the proposition. But now visualize the shutting out as a mechanical process: the model actually moves into the space which had been reserved for the realization of the possibility *not-p*. Next suppose that the space reserved for the realization of the possibility *p* is everywhere else. Then the space in which this particular model operates will be divided exhaustively into two, the p-reserve and the not-p-reserve. So when the model denies the not-p-reserve to reality, it forces it into the p-reserve: 'not-not-p' is logically equivalent to 'p'.

This is not Wittgenstein's only way of using the idea of logical space in the *Tractatus*, but it is his basic way of using it. It can, of course, be translated into two dimensions, in which case the 'Bild' will be what is ordinarily meant by 'a picture', but it is easier to begin with its application to three-dimensional models. It gives an intuitively satisfying account of the way in which an ordinary factual proposition operates: the claim made against reality by the proposition 'p' shows it the door out of the not-p-reserve in the appropriate logical space, and thereby forces it into the p-reserve.

So the idea of 'shutting out' is part of the development of Y. But is this any more than an elaborate analogy? Does it contain any point of substance, or is it merely a way of presenting familiar truths in paint and powder?

Y has always proved difficult to interpret, partly because of its brilliant surface, and partly because most of the points of substance which it contains were worked out by Wittgenstein before he thought of assimilating propositions to pictures. Here it must be remembered that he came to philosophy through the work done on the foundations of logic by Frege and Russell. For the points of substance contained in Y were all either taken over by him from Frege or Russell, or worked out by him as criticisms and modifications of their doctrines. Since most of these ideas came to him before he thought of Y, the content of Y is the nucleus of the system of the *Tractatus*.

The question which Y was to answer is the question how a factual proposition acquires its sense. Part of Y's answer is that somewhere in its analysis words must represent existing things. Now it must be noted that, according to Y, what is represented must exist. For this is the first point of substance in Y: the relation between a word and what it represents is like the relation between a proper name and its bearer. Later, in *Philosophical Investigations*, Wittgenstein singles out this point for criticism.

Valid or not, how exactly did he use this point in the *Tractatus*? Part of this question has already been answered: he used it to establish the linkage with reality through which a factual proposition acquires its sense. But there is a difficulty here. Names by themselves do not say anything. How then can it possibly come about that, when they are combined in a proposition, which is only a concatenation of names, they do say something?

The dramatic answer to this question is the strongly visualized account of shutting out which has already been given. But inside this account there are two more points of substance which have yet to be isolated. First, Wittgenstein maintained that there is no possible way of construing a proposition as a compound name. For there is movement within a proposition, and this movement has a certain direction, or sense. It is worth observing that, before he thought of the mechanical analogy, he illustrated this point from the theory of electricity: a proposition has two poles, one positive and the other negative, and its truth or falsity depends on whether its current flows with reality or against it. But this analogy is in various ways less satisfactory than the mechanical one.

The last point of substance in Y is the most important one. It is that a name is not a complete and self-sufficient semantic unit, like a label or tag. If names were like labels, the question, how by merely putting them together we could produce a proposition which says something, would be unanswerable. But, according to Y, they are not mere labels. Certainly we can think of them in isolation, and it is even true that they have their meanings in isolation, their meanings being the objects with which they are individually correlated. But this truth has to be qualified. When we think of a name in isolation, we have to think of it as something which must be combined with some other name, and perhaps also as something which must not be combined with certain other names. For a name is an abstraction from a proposition, and, since a proposition is a semantic fact, a name is an element abstracted from a semantic fact.

A name is not an *objet trouvé*, which may be put in any spatial context, and so, when it is considered in isolation, is an abstraction from any spatial fact. A name is an abstraction from a semantic fact. So when we think of it in isolation, we must take it together with its necessities of combination with other names. It is, therefore, a mistake to regard a name as something static. Its contribution to the kind of movement which a proposition makes is written into it from the beginning.

One more step is needed to complete this development of Y. For there is still the question, from what source these necessities are derived. Wittgenstein's answer is that they reflect the necessities governing the combinations of the objects with which the names are correlated. So propositions are pictures constructed according to, and therefore reflecting, the necessities which govern the structure of reality. These necessities limit the total space of possibilities within which the actual structure of reality takes shape. In this space a proposition makes a movement which shuts certain possibilities out of their reserves, and thereby forces the realization of certain others. The movement is a legitimate one only because the proposition has already absorbed the relevant necessities into itself. This is how a proposition acquires and uses its sense, and this is the fundamental point of analogy between a proposition and a picture or model.

Wittgenstein's early theory of logical necessity is derived from Y. A factual proposition shuts out some but not all of the possibilities on its list. But a factual proposition is only one of the three kinds of truth-function. There are also tautologies, which shut out none of the listed possibilities, and contradictions, which shut out all of them. The tautology 'p or not-p' is always true, because what it shuts out is nothing. For 'p' is the only proposition in its analysis, and 'p or not-p' will be true whether 'p' is true or 'p' is false. The contradiction 'p and not-p' is never true, because what it shuts out is everything. For again the only proposition in its analysis is 'p', and 'p and not-p' will be false whether 'p' is true or 'p' is false. Tautologies and contradictions are the two limiting cases of truth-functions. A contradiction tries to move into the whole of the relevant logical space, and a tautology leaves the whole of it empty.

It follows that tautologies and contradictions lack factual sense. But though they lack it, they express the necessary connections between other propositions which do not lack it. An argument is valid if the combination of its premisses with its conclusion is a tautology: given the premisses, the conclusion must be true. For example, it is tautological to say that, given 'p', and given 'if p, then q', 'q' will be true. To put the same point negatively, an argument is valid if the combination of its premisses with the negation of its conclusion produces a contradiction.

This is a beautifully simple theory of logical necessity. Taken together with the theory of elementary propositions it provides a uniform explanation of all the necessary truths which people actually use. Naturally, the explanation does not cover the necessary truths of Wittgenstein's own system. But given the theory of elementary propositions, it can be extended to cover all necessary truths which are built into ordinary descriptive words, and can be elicited by logical analysis. For if that theory is correct, the explanation of a necessary truth of this kind will always be that the relevant descriptive word is definable. For example, the word 'crooked' can be defined as 'not straight', and this definition can be used in a very simple way to reduce the necessary truth that, if a thing is crooked it is not straight, to a tautology. The point at which this extension of the explanation of necessary truth might be doubted, has already been indicated: it is dubious whether the necessary truth, that if a thing is blue it is not yellow, really depends on analytical definitions of the colour-words which have yet to be discovered. But the advantage of extending the explanation, if it could be done, is plain. It would yield a uniform theory of all necessary truth. All sources of necessity would be exhibited in the structure of language, and there would be no sources of necessity which had to be left unanalysed in the natures of particular things.

4 Beyond

Wittgenstein's theory of logical necessity is so elegant that it attracts all the attention, and his next step sometimes goes unnoticed. His next step is to argue that, though the propositions of logic are tautologies and not substantial theories, the fact that logic exists does indicate something about the nature of reality: it presupposes the necessary truth that reality consists ultimately of simple objects, or, leaving the qualifications to be understood, of objects. This necessary truth is substantial, and it cannot be reduced to a tautology. So although he leaves no sources of necessity unanalysed in the natures of particular things, he allows that this entirely general necessary truth about reality cannot be analysed out in the usual way.

His argument for this connection between the existence of logic and his ontology can be broken down into stages, some of which have already been traversed. The existence of logic depends on the possibility of combining factual propositions to form tautologies. But that requires the possibility of first constructing factual propositions without which there would be nothing to combine; and this, in its turn, involves the possibility of elementary propositions, and the ultimate granulation of reality. Read in this direction the argument is a transcendental one, which in the spirit of Kant seeks to show how the *a priori* propositions of logic are possible. From this point the argument can be traced back in the reverse direction, from objects to elementary propositions and thence, by the application of the truth-functional formula, to the limit of language, which is fixed by the possible permutations and combinations of elementary propositions, however much this may be disguised by the convenient grossness of factual discourse.

So there is a close connection between the two main tasks which Wittgenstein undertook in the *Tractatus*, the investigation of the foundations of logic, with which the *Notebooks* begins, and the fixing of the limit of language, which is the task emphasized in his Preface to the *Tractatus*. The connection is that logic covers everything that can be said in advance of experience, everything that is *a priori*. Experience can only give us a world of facts, but this world floats in a space of possibilities which is given *a priori*. When logic discloses the structure of factual discourse, it also discloses the structure of reality which factual discourse reflects. These two structures, which are really one, may be regarded as a framework, or grid of co-ordinates, spreading through the whole space of possibilities in which the world of facts floats. The limit of this space, which is reflected in the limit of factual discourse, is determined by logic. For the point of origin from which the limit is calculated is plotted by logic, and the formula by which it is calculated is a logical formula.

It may seem surprising that logic should reveal the essential structure of reality if the propositions of logic are tautologies, and lack factual sense. How can something which is empty have a content? But Wittgenstein does not suggest that tautologies say anything about reality. His suggestion is that the fact that, when certain factual propositions are combined, a tautology is produced, indicates the essential structure of reality. This structure is something which can only be shown.

But why, it might be asked, does he confine this suggestion to tautologies? Why does he not extend it to necessary truths which depend on the definitions of descriptive words, and say that they too show something about the essential nature of reality? There would be three things wrong with the suggested extension. First, the adoption of a certain definition of a descriptive word is always optional, and, where there is a choice, the necessity which the choice produces will only be conditional. Secondly, from the fact that language contains a descriptive word defined in a certain way no conclusion about reality follows, because there might not be anything answering to the description. Thirdly, even from the fact that language contained a certain pure name it could not be inferred that the object named existed necessarily. Certainly, its existence would be conditionally necessary, the condition being the existence of the name. But it would not be unconditionally necessary. Logic only settles what can be said in advance. It cannot settle the question, what objects exist, or the question, what types of object exist, because the answers to these questions would be, at best, only conditionally necessary, and so experience would be needed to settle them.

Behind all these conditional necessities, which depend on the way in which language happens to have developed, Wittgenstein saw one very general unconditional necessity. According to him, the general framework of any factual language is fixed objectively in advance. This framework is a truth-functional structure based on elementary propositions. When human beings devise a particular factual language, they must connect it up to this pre-existing structure. They have certain options about the ways in which they make the connections, but the structure itself is rigid.

The *Tractatus* is a philosophical study of this structure, and the medium through which it works is logic. This explains why the book contains so little detailed analysis of particular types of proposition. Wittgenstein was concerned with the general theory of factual language, and with the general theory of reality which he believed that he could deduce from it. By comparison the details of particular analyses seemed unimportant, because the necessities which they revealed could only be conditional.

But what is the status of the general theory of language, and of the ontology which was deduced from it? This question can now be resumed at the point at which it was left before the detailed account of the system of the *Tractatus* was given. Must it be concluded that these two theories are substantial necessary truths of a Kantian kind, or does the doctrine of showing offer a genuine alternative to this conclusion?

A firm answer to this question can now be extracted from the detailed account of the system. If the two theories were not substantial necessary truths that would be because they were, like Solipsism, deep tautologies. According to Wittgenstein, what the Solipsist offers is a piece of good metaphysics. He expresses the valid point that factual discourse is limited from the inside, because the base on which it is constructed is what exists. His mistake is that he gives this point the wrong kind of expression. He ought to allow it to be shown in the avowed tautology 'What is reflected in the mirror of language is reflected in the mirror of language', or, more simply, 'There is what there is'. These would be deep tautologies, because there is something beneath them which is trying to get out and find a different kind of expression. The Solipsist's mistake is to give it the kind of expression that it wants, by casting it in the form of a substantial necessary truth about what does exist.

Now the question is, whether the thesis, that objects must exist, can be treated in the same way. The answer is that it cannot, because it really is meant as a substantial thesis about the character of what does exist. If it were transformed into a tautology, the tautology would be 'Reality has the character that it has', which was not Wittgenstein's point. He was trying to make the point that reality must have a certain character which he specified. But why must it have this specific character? Because the essential nature of language indicates that it must have it. But how is the essential nature of language discovered? And, however it is discovered, what is the status of the propositions which describe it?

It is clear that these questions cannot be avoided by giving Wittgenstein's theories the transcendental treatment which he gave Solipsism. His theories cannot be treated as deep tautologies. Now a natural way of answering the questions would be to say that either language may be defined, or its nature may be investigated empirically, and that the first of these two alternatives will yield an empty necessary truth, while the second will yield a substantial contingent truth. The Kantian way between the horns of this dilemma was to argue that there are substantial necessary truths. If there is another way between them, it certainly is not indicated by Wittgenstein's doctrine of showing. There is, then, something wrong with this doctrine, or at least with the way in which he applies it to philosophy. What is wrong with it is that it offers the false hope of a non-Kantian way between the horns of the dilemma. Now the doctrine of showing is the semantic aspect of Wittgenstein's so-called 'mysticism' : there are things which cannot be said, but only shown. So when he claimed in a letter to Russell[1] that his doctrine of showing was important, he was right. If it had opened up a new way between the horns of the old dilemma, that would have been an important achievement. But it did not open up a new way, and the doubts which Russell expresses about it in his Introduction to the *Tractatus* were well founded.

Wittgenstein's other applications of the doctrine of showing, to religion, morality and aesthetics, are at first sight very different. It is hard to see anything more than a negative point of analogy with the way in which he applies it to philosophy. The negative point is that, according to him, all four lie outside factual discourse. But what else do they have in common?

A natural answer would be that philosophy has nothing else in common with the other three. In order to see how natural this answer is, it is only necessary to recall the

1. *Notebooks 1914–1916*, Appendix III, p. 130.

predicament in which the critical philosopher's treatment of speculative metaphysics puts religion and morality. The withdrawal of pseudo-scientific support leaves them like stranded leviathans, enormously important but dubiously viable. Obviously it is no good trying to settle their claim to be directly based on material of their own by using the formula which was proposed for philosophy. For religion and morality are certainly not critiques of any further modes of thought. Any attempt to preserve them must allow them their independence. This is what makes the task so difficult.

But it is an important task for reasons which have nothing to do with pure philosophy. Wittgenstein even said that the point of the *Tractatus* was ethical, and that the more important part of the book was the part that he did not write.[2] He meant that, among the things that cannot be said, those which he did not even try to put into words, religion, morality and aesthetics, are more important than the one that he did try to put into words, philosophy. From this point of view, which is, of course, not the point of view of pure philosophy, what makes the demarcation of the limit of factual discourse important is that it prevents encroachment and preserves the three from discrediting pseudo-scientific treatment. It would, of course, be a mistake to infer from this that what Wittgenstein did say in the *Tractatus* seemed to him to have no intrinsic importance.

Preserving religion and morality from this kind of encroachment is not sufficient. It is not enough that there should be a place where they are not to be found. Something more positive is needed. Wittgenstein's doctrine of showing at first sight seems not to meet this need. But in fact it is associated with an important idea which does go some way towards meeting it.

2. *Letters from Ludwig Wittgenstein with a Memoir*: Paul Engelmann: Blackwell, 1967, pp. 143-4. See Biographical Note p. 185.

This idea, which has already been mentioned, is the idea that the world of facts can be seen as a whole. The *Tractatus* is an attempt to say about all possible facts something which cannot really be said, because it is not itself factual, but which can be discerned through the world of facts. There is here a positive analogy between philosophy and religion. For the religion at which Wittgenstein hints in his early writings is a form of pantheism. In the *Tractatus* he says that God does not reveal himself in the world, and this means that he does not reveal himself in any particular fact or set of facts. In the *Notebooks* he goes further and says that God is the world. So the object of philosophical inquiry is also the object of religious feelings. But though the object is the same, it is approached in two different ways, and there is no suggestion that the logic and ontology of the *Tractatus* are a form of theology.

It is not easy to see how this idea can be extended to morality and art. Since Wittgenstein says less about art, the general shape of his shadowy doctrine may best be seen from the way in which he tries to extend it to morality. He points out that, if any kind of thing has intrinsic value, it is not a contingent fact that it has it. Nor, of course, is it an ordinary tautology. So an ascription of intrinsic value would seem to have the same puzzling character that he found in Solipsism and in other metaphysical theories: it would seem to be a substantial necessary truth. Can it then be vindicated in the same way, as an attempt to say about the world of facts, taken as a whole, something which, though valid, cannot be said? But what ascriptions of intrinsic value could be interpreted in this way? At this point the trail of ideas becomes fainter. He is inclined to say that happiness alone is intrinsically good. Moreover, he seems to think that this ascription of intrinsic value to happiness does contain a valid point about the world of facts seen as a whole. For, according to him, to be happy is to see the world of facts as a whole with expanding limits, whereas an unhappy man would feel that the same limits, enclosing the same facts, were pressing in on him. If it is the happy man's view of the world which alone has intrinsic value, it is perhaps understandable that the ascription of intrinsic value to it should neither be a tautology nor a factual proposition about anything in his world, but, rather, a transcendental judgement. Although it would be true that his world had a certain character, he could not express this truth as a substantial thesis, but only as a deep tautology.

But when happiness in construed in this way, how is it connected with ordinary human actions? Wittgenstein had no complete answer to this question. He pointed out that it is not logically necessary that willing should produce the action willed. So if the intrinsic value of good willing accrued to it from the actions willed, it would belong to it contingently. But since intrinsic value never belongs to any kind of thing contingently, the intrinsic value of good willing, if it has any, cannot accrue to it from the actions willed. Moreover, if we try to identify the kind of willing which could have intrinsic value non-contingently and non-tautologically, we find that it always recedes into the background, leaving nothing but its contingent consequences to be recorded, just as the metaphysical subject receded into the background, leaving nothing but its thoughts and experiences to be recorded. When all these contingent consequences have been rejected as irrelevant, we are driven to the conclusion that, if any will has intrinsic value, it is not the psychological will that has it, but the transcendental will, which, like the metaphysical subject, is not a part of the world. But does any will have intrinsic value? Wittgenstein suggests that it does, and hints that the good will is happiness.

Here again many of the ideas are Schopenhauer's, but, though Wittgenstein begins to use them in his own way, his line of thought is not fully worked out. However, two points can be made about it. First, whatever the exact positive analogy that he saw between philosophy and ethics, it is obvious that he did not think that a philosophical investigation of language would lead to any conclusions in ethics. Secondly, though he like Kant wished to keep ethics safe from the encroachments of science, there is a striking difference between their ethical views. Kant tried to establish that certain ethical theses, which can be applied to ordinary human life and action, are substantial necessary truths. This kind of solution was not open to Wittgenstein. Nor was it possible for him to treat value judgements as factual propositions or as ordinary tautologies. So he gave them the transcendental treatment which he gave to Solipsism and other metaphysical theories. He insisted that they must have the kind of necessity which can scarcely be accommodated in his system, and so he priced his ethical theory out of this world.

Part 2

Wittgenstein's Later Philosophy

5 The Task

In his Preface to *Philosophical Investigations*, Wittgenstein says that it seemed to him that he ought to include a reissue of the *Tractatus* in the same volume, because his new thoughts could be seen in the right light only by contrast with, and against the background of, his old thoughts.[1] He did not merely want to emphasize the fact that his new thinking is startlingly different in character. If that had been all, he could have ignored the past and started afresh. His point was that, in spite of the differences between his early work and his later work, what he was trying to do was still the same kind of thing, and that the change in method was not a sharp break with the past, but a gradual transformation of the ideas of the *Tractatus* which preserved what was good in them. So he placed a sympathetic critique of those ideas at the beginning of *Philosophical Investigations*.

It is only too easy to get lost in the details of his later work. So some account of his new conception of the philosopher's task and of his new method will be given first. This will serve as an introduction to a more detailed discussion of some of his later contributions to philosophy.

His task was still to plot the limit of language, but he had come to take a different view of what this task involved. He had ceased to expect the limit to be one continuous line. For factual discourse no longer held pride of place on the drawing board, and, when he did concentrate on it, he found that he was not really able to derive its rich variety of different forms from a single essence. So there would be

1. This plan could not be carried out in the edition of the book which includes an English translation.

many points of origin and many subdivisions of logical space. His task, as he now saw it, was to relate these subdivisions to one another by drawing the network of lines between them.

It might seem that this task is totally different from the task which he had set himself in his Preface to the *Tractatus*, and that it is only the imagery which creates the illusion that it is a different conception of the same task. For in what way would this filigree of lines resemble the single sweeping line of the *Tractatus*? Surely the line of the *Tractatus* was meant to be the external limit of language, with nothing outside it, whereas the new lines would mark internal subdivisions. What then has happened to the outer limit? Has it any counterpart in the new scheme of things? At least it seems clear that if there is a counterpart, it cannot be the system of internal lines.

But beneath these differences there is something which remains the same. For when he said in his Preface to the *Tractatus* that there is nothing outside the limit of language, he meant that there is nothing factual outside the limit of factual language. He allowed that there are also things which cannot be said in factual propositions, but which can be shown. Now these factually unsayable things belong to other kinds of discourse, the most important kinds, judged from a standpoint outside philosophy, being religious, moral and aesthetic. So, on the ordinary vague view of these other kinds of discourse, though there would be nothing factual outside the limit of factual discourse, it might look as if there would not therefore be nothing outside it, and so the line drawn in the *Tractatus* could be regarded as an internal line.

But this will not really do. For in the *Tractatus* Wittgenstein did not take an ordinary vague view of these other kinds of discourse. He offered an extraordinary transcendental analysis of them. So when he said that beyond the line of demarcation which he drew in the *Tractatus* there must be silence, he did not merely mean that there must be scientific silence. He meant that any attempt to put non-scientific truths into words would necessarily distort them by forcing them into the mould of scientific discourse. So religion, ethics and aesthetics, like the philosophy of the *Tractatus*, all slide into the limbo reserved for transcendental subjects, because factual discourse really does occupy the dominant position—indeed, the only position. It would, therefore, be a mistake to regard the line drawn in the *Tractatus* as an internal line. But what one can say here, in order to bring out the continuity in Wittgenstein's conception of his task, is that the pressure exerted by those other kinds of discourse was going to change the map of logical space. In the *Tractatus* he had pushed them off the map, not, of course, in any intolerant positivistic way, but in a subtle, sympathetic, transcendental way, and at least two of them, ethics and aesthetics, seem not to be amenable to this treatment.

There were also strong disruptive pressures within the logical space of factual discourse. For his early theory of factual propositions was a theory about their essence, and so he did not pay much attention to the specific differences between the various forms of factual proposition. There were two distinct dangers here. First, the so-called 'essence', which was the centre of interest, might have no better claim to recognition than the specific differences which were neglected. Secondly, it might not really be the essence, because a closer look at the different varieties might reveal that it was not really shared by all of them.

Wittgenstein came to think that his early theory of factual discourse suffered from both these faults. It showed a contempt for the particular case which was unjustified in itself and led to a false generalization. He might, perhaps, have been expected to try to correct the second fault by looking for a better account of the essence of factual discourse. But by that time he had come to the conclusion that it was no good looking for the essence, because there was nothing worthy of that title there to be found. There was only a crowd of differing, but variously related forms of factual propositions. So a network of internal lines began to spread over what had been the homogeneous logical space of factual discourse.

Something has already been said about the way in which he came to give up his early theory of language. One by one he rejected all the axioms and assumptions on which it was based. Z was the first to go, and its fate will be described in some detail later, because it is a very clear stage on the route from the *Tractatus* to *Philosophical Investigations*.

The other fault was, of course, inevitable in the *Tractatus*. A philosopher bent on the quest for the essence of all factual propositions could not see any interest in the specific differences between their various forms. However, it must not be forgotten that Wittgenstein's later respect for the particular case, and the consequent diversification of the logical space of factual discourse, both develop out of something which is already in the *Tractatus*. For one of the tasks which was there assigned to the philosopher was analysis of the kind practised by Russell and Moore. This task may seem unimportant when it is compared with the task of drawing a line around the whole of factual discourse, but it is there, in the *Tractatus*, unequivocally assigned to the philosopher. Naturally, the examples of this kind of analysis which are given in the *Tractatus* are all related to Wittgenstein's own theory of factual discourse. For his whole endeavour was to prove that, however striking the specific differences between the various forms of factual propositions may be, they can all be reduced to elementary propositions. But it is easy to see how this kind of analysis might become disinterested, or rather how the interest might spread. It took attention off the outer limit of factual discourse, and turned it onto the network of internal boundaries.

This line of development may be illustrated by two examples, one from the *Tractatus*, and the other a very simplified illustration of the kind of thing that Wittgenstein was trying to do in his later period. In the *Tractatus* he mentions the importance of analysing the difference between the 'is' of identity in such a sentence as 'This is the man who fired the shot', and the 'is' of predication in such a sentence as 'This man is too tall'. But though the details of this difference are interesting and difficult, he rushes through them with one purpose in mind: to prove that contingent identity statements can be analysed in a way that does not conflict with his theory of factual discourse.

The second example will illustrate the kind of thing which he does in his later work. It has already been mentioned that he deliberately left it an open question whether the objects of the *Tractatus* would be material or phenomenological, because for his purpose it did not matter. But suppose that we were analysing ascriptions of sensations and ascriptions of material possessions to people, and suppose that our interest in the two analyses was not related to any particular philosophical theory. We would soon come across a striking difference between the kinds of questions that can be asked about material objects and the kinds of questions that can be asked about sensations. The question, 'Could A have had the sensation that B is now having?' cannot be meant in the same way as the question 'Could A have had the car that B now has?'

We cannot mean the first question in this way, because, if we tried to mean it in this way, we would be transgressing an internal boundary between two areas of factual discourse. We may, of course, mean to ask whether A could have had another sensation like the one that B is now having, but we cannot mean to ask whether he could have had the very same sensation that B is now having; or, rather, we cannot mean this question as one to which the correct answer might happen to be 'Yes' or might happen to be

'No'. This impossibility is the consequence of the lack of a suitable criterion of identity. A car can be identified when it leaves the factory, and then it is a contingent question whether it was bought by A or B, and, if it was bought by B, it is another contingent question whether it could have been bought by A instead: for example, could A have afforded it? But neither the ascription nor the identification of sensations works like this, and so we could not possibly mean the original question about B's sensation in the same way as the question about B's car. If we tried to mean it in this way, we would be trying to achieve an impossible conceptual feat. We would be trying to cross an internal boundary between two areas of factual discourse without really crossing it. The area in which we start is the area of discourse about sensations, and we would be trying to cross over into the area of discourse about material objects without crossing over completely, as if we hoped that the boundary line had some magnitude, so that we could take an ambiguous stand on it.

But, it might be asked, where in all this is the sameness in Wittgenstein's task? The account which has been given so far certainly shows that there is continuity in the development of his philosophy, but does it not really amount to saying that he substituted a new task for the old one? For drawing boundaries within factual discourse is not the same thing as enclosing it all within a single external boundary, and treating the external boundary as if it had something beyond it is not the same thing as treating it as if it had nothing beyond it. So, however natural it was for Wittgenstein to substitute the first member of each of these pairs for the second, it was in each case the substitution of something entirely different.

So it might seem. But there are still two more questions to be asked about Wittgenstein's conception of philosophy, and the answers to them will demonstrate that his second task really is a new form of his first task. What happens when a boundary is transgressed? And what do the transgressor and the philosopher say to one another afterwards?

The answer to the first question is that in the system of the *Tractatus* someone who transgresses the external boundary of factual discourse produces factual nonsense. Similarly, the idea behind the new philosophy is that someone who transgresses one of its internal boundaries produces factual nonsense. It is true that there is also a difference between the two cases. For in the first case what produces factual nonsense is simply the crossing of the external boundary, whereas in the second case it is produced when someone crosses an internal boundary without completely crossing it. So in the second case the word 'transgress' has a different and more complex meaning. There would be nothing wrong with really crossing an internal boundary, and, for example, using factual discourse about material objects instead of using factual discourse about sensations. The mistake is to try to keep one foot on each side of the boundary, because the two areas of discourse really must be kept distinct from one another. But underneath this difference there is the important similarity that the boundaries mark the points at which there is a danger that factual nonsense might be produced.

The answer to the second question is less obvious but equally important. When the philosopher tells the transgressor that he cannot make that move, the transgressor will ask 'Why not?' In the system of the *Tractatus* the reason given was that there was no place there to move into. The logical space of factual discourse is curved, and outside it there is a super-void, which is not even a matrix of possibilities. But the transgressor is a man who is never satisfied with this explanation. He always imagines that, if he cannot cross the outer boundary, that must be because there is something on the other side which stops him. His idea is that the necessity, that he should stay within the boundary if he is going to produce factual sense, must have some sort of factual backing outside the boundary. He thinks that what creates the necessity must be something on the other side of the boundary which the philosopher ought to be able to describe to him. But the philosopher's point is that he cannot describe any such thing, because description belongs to factual discourse, and beyond its own outer boundary factual discourse must cease. So he can only tell the transgressor that the explanation of the necessity is to be found in what lies within the boundary.

How would the conversation go when what the transgressor does is to try to cross an internal boundary without completely crossing it? Again he will ask the philosopher why he cannot make the move that he wants to make. In Wittgenstein's later work the reason given is that there is nothing in between the two areas of discourse, so that the half move which the transgressor wants to make is not a possibility. The internal boundary is a line without magnitude, and there is no such place as halfway across. But the transgressor is a man who is never satisfied with this explanation. He always imagines that, if he cannot make a half move, that must be because there is something in between which stops him. His idea is that the necessity, that he should stay on one side or the other if he is going to produce factual sense, must have some sort of factual backing. He thinks that what creates this necessity must be something in between the two areas, which the philosopher ought to be able to describe to him. But the philosopher's point is that he cannot describe any such thing, because description belongs to factual discourse, and between its own contiguous areas factual discourse must cease. So he can only tell the transgressor that the explanation of the necessity is to be found in what lies within the two areas.

There are differences between these two conversations. For instance, in the second one there is the complication about what counts as a transgression. But in the second one, as in the first, the transgressor suffers from the illusion that he ought to be able to see through the necessity and discern a factual basis beyond it. In the terminology of the early doctrine, he wants to be told what he can only be shown. In Wittgenstein's two conceptions of the philosopher's task it is an important common factor that this illusion has to be dispelled.

There are two further differences between his early and his later conceptions of the philosopher's task which ought to be mentioned in this introduction to his new philosophy. The first is really a difference of degree. In his later work the idea that philosophy is retrieval is very heavily emphasized: it is natural to transgress, and the philosopher is a good shepherd. This idea, about which more will be said later, is present in the *Tractatus*, but it is less obtrusive, because the theory of language, which was itself to be treated as a transgressor in the later period, occupies the foreground.

The second difference is a matter of philosophical theory rather than a matter of theory about philosophy, but it raises a fundamental question about the nature of philosophy. If we reflect on the ways in which the two conversations went, we can see that there is a further question which the two transgressors might have asked. They might have been persuaded that the necessities in the two cases could not have factual bases in the prohibited non-areas. But they might still have inquired what their precise bases in the permitted areas were. Now in the system of the *Tractatus* the answer given was that the necessity was unconditional, and that its source was a very general objective feature of reality. But in Wittgenstein's later work the question is answered in a very different way: the necessity is conditional, and its source is in us. This shift towards anthropocentrism raises a fundamental question which will be discussed later. If necessities are always conditional, and if they are deposits laid down in language by human beings, then will not the philosopher's task merely be to uncover these deposits, so that philosophy will become a branch of science? Of course, it will be a rather unusual science, a sort of anthropological study of conceptual systems, but still it will be a science. To put the point in another way, there will be only one tenable philosophical theory, the theory which in the earlier discussion of religion and ethics was called 'the subtle kind of positivism'. The philosopher's last word will always be ·That is how people are. They think and speak in the ways that I have described.'

6   The Method

Wittgenstein's new method developed when he applied his early critique of language to itself. Now the theory of language behind the early critique was based on a small set of intuitions about the essence of factual discourse. These intuitions were supposed to be substantial necessary truths, but it was difficult to see how any substantial necessary truths could be accommodated within the early theory of language or how they could have been established in the first place. He attempted to meet the first difficulty by giving them a transcendental status. But though this treatment might be appropriate to Solipsism, and perhaps to certain other metaphysical theories, it was not appropriate to his early theory of language. His reaction to the second difficulty is harder to discern, because he theorized on such an exalted plane, far above the ordinary human phenomenon of actual language from which he must have started. His account of elementary propositions was supported by an elaborate deduction, but surely the premisses of this deduction, X, Y and Z, ought at least to have fitted actual language, whatever higher aspirations they may have had. So when he came to the conclusion that they do not fit actual language, he abandoned them and the method which had led to them. That method is often called 'essentialism'.

The only other points that have been made so far about the new method are that it is empirical, as its origin suggests; that it shows great respect for the particular case; and that it is more like art than science, because the nuances of particular cases are not caught in any theory, but are presented in careful descriptions of actual linguistic practices, and by brilliant collocations of examples. But how are these points connected with one another? Do they really amount to the delineation of a new method, or is it, perhaps, the absence of a method? And whatever name is given to this new style of thinking, what could it contribute to philosophy?

The description of the new method needs to be expanded and illustrated. Perhaps it would be best to begin with the negative points. In this introductory account there is no need to go into Wittgenstein's precise reasons for rejecting X, Y and Z. The important point is the general one. X, Y and Z are examples of essentialist theses about language, and essentialist theses about language are themselves examples of one type of metaphysical thinking. For according to critical philosophers, the general characteristic of metaphysical thinking is that it loses contact with its material. Now there are really two distinct contact-breaking moves: intuitive generalizing about the material, which is what the essentialist does, and extrapolating the results into a void. What Kant criticized in speculative metaphysics was often the second contact-breaking move: for example, the concept of a cause ought not to be extrapolated beyond the limits of phenomena. Later philosophers criticized Kant himself for making the first contact-breaking move: it ought not to be assumed that causality is a universal feature of all phenomena. What Wittgenstein criticized in the *Tractatus* was the extrapolation of factual language beyond its limits. He became his own critic later, when he treated the theory of language of the *Tractatus* as an intuitive generalization which does not fit actual language.

His later view was that he had made two distinct mistakes at this point. First, the generalization was not the result of an empirical investigation of language. As far as this point goes, he might have been expected to try to find a better account of the essence of language. But in fact, as has already been mentioned, he did not try to do this. He changed the whole direction of his inquiry, because he believed that he had made a second mistake. He had wrongly assumed that the multifarious uses of language must have a high common factor. The truth was more complex: each resembled others in many different ways, like the faces of people belonging to the same family, or like human games. Naturally, if the description of the essence were allowed to include alternatives, there would still be an essence to be found. But the whole point of essentialism was that the common factor was supposed not to include alternatives. In that case, Wittgenstein objected, it was a mistake to assume that the common factor would be high enough to be of any interest, and he turned his investigation onto the multitudinous differences.

So when he rejected the essentialist theory of the *Tractatus*, he was at the same time doing something much more general. He was abandoning the old, high, *a priori* investigation and starting something quite different in its place, an investigation of the human phenomenon of language which would be empirical, pedestrian and even homely.

This development was also helped in a second way by his attack on essentialism. He directed his attack not only against his own early theory of languages, but also against the practice of the common type of analysis which is recommended in the *Tractatus*. That type of analysis always sought definitions. But to suppose that a meaning can always be caught in a definition is to make one of the two mistakes which he diagnosed in essentialism: it is to assume that the things to which the word is applied have a high common factor, and that they are not merely related to one another like the faces of members of the same family. It ought to be noted that he qualified this criticism in a way in which he did not qualify his other criticism, that the multitudinous uses of languages have no high common factor. For naturally he allowed that the meaning of a word can sometimes be caught in a definition, but he did not admit that the word 'language' is a case of this kind.

In order to gauge the effect of this second anti-essentialist move, it is only necessary to see how much would be omitted from an account of the differences and resemblances between the various things that people say, if that account were only allowed to include definitions and logical equivalences. For example, there would be no mention of differences between speech-acts: an expression of pain is something quite different from a careful description of a pain given to a doctor. Or, to revert to an example used earlier, there is a difference between the criterion of identity of a sensation and the criterion of identity of a material object, but these criteria of identity would not naturally be included in the definitions of 'sensation' and 'material object'.

When the two moves against essentialism are combined, the effect is prodigious. Philosophy, in the form of a critique of language, is brought down from the sky, and planted firmly on the ground. Any ordinary fact about language could be relevant.

But to what would it be relevant? It would be relevant to Wittgenstein's new task, the drawing of the network of boundaries, which, according to him, have to be drawn within language. But this part of the answer is easy. There is no difficulty in seeing that the method is appropriate to the task set. The difficulty begins when we inquire how the task set can fail to be a scientific task, if it is to be carried out in this way. For if philosophical answers are based on ordinary empirical facts about language, then will not philosophical questions be ordinary factual questions about language? If philosophy can be done in this way, will it not be absorbed into the science of linguistics? Up to this point philosophy, even in its critical form, had somehow succeeded in preserving its own special status. It had survived as a non-scientific subject on the fringe of ordinary science, like the Celts. But its independent survival appeared to have been achieved only by an adaptation which was now being abandoned. The successful adaptation was the claim to be able to record absolute necessities of a special kind, which were neither unsupportable, like the absolute necessities of speculative metaphysics, nor, of course, empirically supported, like scientific results. But this claim was now being abandoned, and the independent status of philosophy seemed to be inevitably compromised.

When the claim is abandoned, there seems to be nothing left for the philosopher to do except to record conditional necessities which depend on contingent facts about language. For example, it is no doubt an important fact that we have no criterion of identity for sensations that would enable us to answer the question 'Could A have had the sensation which B is now having?', when this question is meant in the way that was explained earlier; but it is still only a contingent fact. For we could invent a new criterion of identity for sensations which would fill the gap, and, if someone objected that it would have to be a very artificial criterion of identity, that too would only be a contingent fact. Whenever the answer is factual, the question must have been factual too. Therefore, philosophy becomes a science.

One reaction to this predicament would be to accept the conclusion that philosophy is a sort of science. Some philosophers would accept it, others try to avoid it but cannot see how to avoid it, and some scientists would welcome it. Another reaction would be to maintain that there are limits to anthropocentrism and the subtle kind of positivism that goes with it, and that philosophy can still maintain itself as an independent inquiry into a system of objective necessities within which our linguistic options are exercised. The philosophy of logic is the area in which this kind of systematic work usually starts. For it is, of course, possible to treat logical necessity as something absolute and objective without drawing the ontological conclusions which Wittgenstein drew in the *Tractatus*. There is also another area in which the foundations of systematic philosophy are sometimes laid. It is possible to argue that certain categorial concepts, such as the concept of a material object, or a sensation, or a person, are objectively linked together in ways which do not depend on us, and that these linkages form a rigid framework within which we have a certain amount of free play.

However, Wittgenstein did not react to the predicament in any of these three ways. He abandoned the claim that philosophy is an inquiry into an objective system of absolute necessities; and yet he did not draw the conclusion that it must, therefore, be a sort of science. He maintained that the right method in philosophy is to collect facts about language, but not because of their own intrinsic interest, nor in order to construct some scientific theory about them, such as a theory about the common grammatical structure of all languages. The facts are to be collected because they point beyond themselves. They point back in the direction from which critical philosophy has travelled in the last two centuries. They have, therefore, a significance which cannot be caught in any scientific theory. They are the conductors through which the feelings and aspirations of pre-critical philosophy are to be earthed. The task of collecting them and arranging them is more like the work of an artist than a scientist.

Wittgenstein's claim, that philosophy can look like a science without being a science, raises three important questions. Does his philosophy justify the claim? Can it be justified? And is his way of doing philosophy the only correct way? Our main concern will be with the first question. If the answer to it is affirmative, then, of course, the answer to the second one will be affirmative too. But it would not follow that there are no other legitimate ways of doing philosophy. However, very little will be said about the third question.

It must be observed that the second question is much more than an academic question of classification; how the books ought to be arranged on the shelves. It is a crucial question in the history of ideas, and, since every student of philosophy recapitulates this part of the history of ideas in his own thoughts, it becomes a personal question : 'What do I think about this?'

It is partly through Wittgenstein's work that the question, in this form, has become inescapable. For his later philosophy gets into people's lives. The *Tractatus* has the kind of aloof beauty which is admired from a distance, like ancient Egyptian architecture. Of course, it raises the very question which is here being discussed, but it raises it in a less human, and less easily recognizable form. It is too abstract, and its doctrines are too difficult to understand. But the later philosophy really works its way into people's lives. It is not that it necessarily makes converts of them, but rather that, when it does persuade them, that is the right description of their state, and that, when it does not persuade them, the opposite reaction is equally strong. It has a powerful magnetic field of attraction and repulsion.

To assess the effects of a philosophy is always a complex task. One explanation of the wide influence, both positive and negative, exerted on philosophers by Wittgenstein's later work is that the question which it raises in an acute form, whether philosophy can avoid being a science, was already very much in the air. It also raises the more general question of the scope and limits of science and its possible encroachments on other fields besides philosophy, and this question has been with all of us for an equally long time. Even if we confine ourselves to philosophical method, there is another point which ought to be made here. Many readers of Wittgenstein's later works would answer the first of the three questions in the affirmative, and with passion : he does justify his claim to have brought philosophy down to earth without turning it into a science. If they are right, the effect is extraordinary. The old feelings and aspirations no longer discharge themselves in treatises which few can understand. They are somehow connected with familiar facts, which are presented in short, sharp observations, interspersed with arresting questions, and startling dialectical *volte-faces*. Personal involvement cannot be avoided, and the old style of philosophizing has been replaced by something fresh and accessible, and perhaps, once it has been tried, irresistible.

There are other explanations of Wittgenstein's spell. There is the extraordinary force of his personal teaching, which is something which cannot be wholly understood apart from his life and character, and there are his achievements outside philosophy, which are like those of some figure of the Renaissance.[1] But our concern here is not with the question why his influence was so great; but rather, granted that one explanation of his influence was that he seemed to have brought philosophy down to earth without turning it into a science, we want to know whether this was an illusion or a fact.

If it was a fact, it was achieved by his theory of transgression and retrieval. For the idea behind this theory is more subtle than it appears to be. At first sight it seems that he is only saying that people tend to confuse different areas of discourse, and to misconstrue something in one area on the analogy with something in another area, like children or savages. But though he does say this, what he means really goes much deeper. He means that certain confusions of this kind point beyond themselves, or at least seem to point beyond themselves to a way out of the familiar areas into the depths of logical space. There are, of course, other, superficially similar confusions, but which do not hold out any such promise of an enlargement of our view into

1. See *Ludwig Wittgenstein, A Memoir*, Norman Malcolm, with *A Biographical Sketch*, Georg Henrik von Wright, Oxford University Press, 1958.

reality. These confusions are gratuitous, shallow and of no philosophical interest. The confusions with which the philosopher ought to concern himself always seem to point into the depths. Now human thought has a natural and almost irresistible tendency to make these confusions, and we feel that there really are hidden depths in the direction indicated by them. The philosopher's task is to show that the depths are illusory. He does this by relentlessly, but at the same time sympathetically, reminding the other (who is an important character in Wittgenstein's later works) of facts about language which he really always knew. These reminders must, of course, be true empirical statements about language, but their significance comes from the background against which they are assembled. The background is the illusion of depth.

An example is needed to illustrate the way in which this method operates. The example which has already been used will serve this purpose, but it will have to be worked out in more detail, so that various threads can be pulled together at this point. The question is 'Could A have had the sensation which B is now having?', and it is meant in the way which has already been explained. Now it must be pointed out that, though the two areas of discourse which are confused in this example are frequently, and perhaps inevitably confused, this particular confusion could only be made by a philosopher. It may seem odd that a philosopher should confuse things which a non-philosopher would not confuse, but there is a reason for this, and it will be explained later.

Meanwhile let us look more closely at the example. The critical philosopher reminds the other, who in this case is also some sort of a philosopher, that there is no criterion of identity for sensations which would enable him to mean the question in the way in which he wants to mean it, as a question to which the answer might happen to be 'Yes', or might happen to be 'No'. What illusion does this reminder dispel? The answer already given to this question is that the illusion which is dispelled consists of two closely linked elements: first, there is the other's idea that he can somehow slip out between the two areas of discourse, and then there is his idea that, if he cannot do so, this must be because there is something between the two areas which stops him. His confusion seems to point beyond itself towards the new and exciting possibility that sensations might really be sent to people, and that they might migrate from one person to another. But even if he is persuaded that these things are necessarily not so, his old confusion may still seem to him to point to something out there—no longer, of course, to a possibility, but to something which creates the impossibility. So the philosopher, having demonstrated the impossibility, must repeat that its source lies within the two areas of discourse, and that it has no deeper backing. The philosopher's part in this conversation is to say things about the two areas which nobody would deny. But in the context of this conversation they are not superficial things. The other's illusions give them depth. But what the other has to realize is that the depth is on the surface.

The original question takes the phrase 'same sensation' beyond the proper limits of its application, and so it runs idle like a disengaged cog. This is a contact-breaking move of the extrapolating kind. For not all extrapolations go across the external boundary of language. Some start from particular words and phrases within it, just as essentialism need not be concerned with the general nature of language, but may be concerned with the nature of something designated by a particular word within it.

Wittgenstein's method of dealing with this kind of extrapolation may seem to be too conservative, because his retrieval of the other always brings him back to the existing structure of discourse, which after all is not sacrosanct. But it was from the existing structure that the other took off, and so the first thing to be done is always to bring him back to it. After that, he may be shown how to modify it, if he really wants to, and there would be a point in showing him this too. For the way to modify the structure is to change it, and not to take it as it is and try to use it as a vehicle for travel outside the logical space of which it is itself the point of origin. And the way to change it is actually to do some work on it.

For example, the other may, if he wishes, lay down a new rule: when two people get what we call the same sensation, *i.e.* two exactly similar sensations, from the same stimulus, say touching a live wire, within the same minute, they have the same sensation in the sense already explained, *i.e.* numerically the same sensation, provided that the two experiences do not overlap in time. A moment's reflection will show that this would be a useless innovation, but that it would succeed in turning the original question into a question about a contingent matter, because the answer would happen to be 'Yes', if A were near the wire at the time, and 'No' if he were too far away. Moreover the new rule allows a sensation to migrate from one person to another. For this would be the way to describe what would happen if B picked up the wire and instantly dropped it, and immediately afterwards A picked it up.

It must be observed that, if this were all that would be meant by 'a migrating sensation' (new style), it would not be very exciting. This is the point of the lesson. What the other really wanted was a case of a sensation actually travelling around from person to person, and perhaps hovering over the wire waiting for someone to come and have it.

How could he have wanted anything so crazy? Material possessions start in factories, are acquired new, and passed on second hand, and they manage all this because they travel soberly in physical space. In what medium could sensations match this performance?

But nothing is too crazy in this kind of drama. For, of course, what the other really wanted could not be put into words that would do justice to it. He is like a man who wakes from a dream mumbling words which made sense in the dream but are now empty. Somewhere in his mind, he feels, there is a very subtle specification of what he wants to say, but he cannot find the right expression for it, and what the philosopher offers him is only a crude parody. If he concentrated on the specification which is really there in his mind, he might succeed in explaining what he wanted to mean by ' a migrating sensation' (old style).

But the philosopher's point is that there is no such thing as 'a migrating sensation' (old style). Or rather, since putting his point in this way might suggest that there is something outside the relevant logical space which blocks the other's move, it would be better to say that for the phrase 'migrating sensation' old style is no style.

There is something in the other's mind, but it is only a vague picture, or perhaps not even that, but only the conviction that it must be possible to construct a picture of the kind that he wants out of the available material. But a dreamer who wakes with the conviction that the dream which he remembers accurately in nonsensical words was in fact a perfectly developed visual sequence, cannot really be right about this. Any construction is limited by the nature of the material used, and if the other wants to construct something which violates the nature of the material, he must first change its nature. He will then have a style, but it will be a new style, and, of course, a disappointment.

In the old imagery of the *Tractatus* what the other wants to do is to extend the logical space of the phrase 'same sensation' without shifting its point of origin. The philosopher counters with a dilemma : either the boundary must be left where it is, or, if it is to be changed, it must really be changed, and that means that its point of origin must be shifted.

It is an important feature of this debate that the philosopher at no point propounds a philosophical theory. For instance, nothing that he has said in the course of the conversation implies materialism. When the other is retrieved it is always to a fact about language that he is retrieved, and never to a theory.

It was this feature of the method which was found perplexing earlier, and provoked the question, how philosophy done in Wittgenstein's new way could avoid becoming a science. The answer given was that, though the facts which are cited are empirical facts about language, they get their philosophical significance from the use to which they are put. They are used to recall the other from his hopeless quest. He is the dupe of confusions which seem to point beyond themselves to ways out of the familiar areas into the depths of logical space. The philosopher brings him back by reminding him of facts which he really always knew.

It may be felt that in the example used to illustrate this kind of drama the philosopher had an easy victory, and that this was because the particular confusion which was chosen was one which nobody would ever make. But in fact it is not true that nobody would make it. What is true is that it would not be made by anyone who had not thought a lot about the philosophical questions how sensations differ from material objects and how the two are related to one another.

If we want to find, in the same general area, an example of a confusion which might be made by someone who had never philosophized in his life, we only have to take the original question and make two changes in it, and ask whether A could acquire B's memories. This new question could be meant in a way which involved confusions roughly similar to those behind the original question, and, if it were meant in such a way, a similar philosophical drama would be played out. But this drama would need a much larger stage, because this time the question of personal identity would come in, and there would be strong human feelings at work. Moreover, at a certain point the plot might take an entirely different turn. For whereas nobody would actually maintain that a sensation might travel around from person to person, the idea, that a particular set of memories, or, more generally, a particular consciousness might leave its body, is one which many would defend, precisely because what would be left behind would not be the person but most probably his corpse. Is it an illusion that these words seem to point beyond the familiar areas of discourse to a real possibility outside them? Where exactly does this part of the boundary of the logical space of factual possibilities run? It is impossible not to be involved in this question, because there is something here which everybody would wish to get clear.

But, to return to the original question, it is not true that nobody would make the confusion that lies behind it. The truth is that it is a confusion that could only occur fairly far along a certain line of philosophical thought. For example, when Hume is developing his system, which is a sort of psychology without bodies, he talks about sensations and ideas as if they could exist before they were combined to form the sets which, according to him, are all that people are. It is true that he realizes that there must be something wrong with this picture, because its consequences are unacceptable, but he never succeeds in showing what is wrong with it. In fact, it is based on the confusion that lay behind our original question. Of course, Hume would never have asked it in real life. But his highly abstract and sophisticated philosophical system rests on the tacit assumption that, if it were asked, it would be a question about a contingent matter. It is this sort of thing that explains how Wittgenstein could achieve so much by merely bringing philosophy back into contact with real life.

He was not the only philosopher to do this. Moore was

another. But whereas what Wittgenstein does can seem magical, this is never true of Moore, however impressive his achievement may be. Yet what Wittgenstein does is not magical, and, if it seems so, that is largely because of the way in which he treats the background against which it is done. The background is always mysterious and shadowed by myth and dream, but what he does against it is always done slowly and visibly.

What he does is invariably to remind the other of the structure of the areas of discourse from which he took off. So the line from which he sets out in pursuit of the other and to which he retrieves him is actual human speech and thought, which may sometimes be supplemented with some workable innovations. Now though this method may seem to have a destructive positivistic tendency, in fact this is not so. For example, it is still his view that religious propositions do not even purport to express factual possibilities. Their meaning, he now thinks, is to be gathered from their place in human life. This is the way in which he would treat the proposition that a person survives the death of his body and is judged by God.

This treatment is a natural application of his new method, and it preserves religious propositions from the encroachments of science. But in certain areas of the philosophy of mind it produces a difficulty, which paradoxically made his work simpler. What is difficult is to draw the line between factual and religious discourse point by point, particularly in a case like the migration of consciousness, which is a tenet with one foot on each side of the line. Wittgenstein's reaction to this difficulty was to rely on his general method of separating the two areas, and he says very little about the detailed dissection of this kind of case. This certainly simplifies his task. But is it really enough to maintain that the religious content of a mixed proposition must not be interpreted factually? Even this might be resisted, and perhaps rightly resisted by the other, who might well feel that every element in a mixed proposition is itself mixed, and that, if this were not so, the proposition would lose its point. He might also find it strange that Wittgenstein can say so much about the alleged factual content of a purely religious proposition and so little about its genuine religious content. His profound reticences were appropriate to the transcendental theory of religion offered in the *Tractatus*, but are they so appropriate to the later treatment?'

Although Wittgenstein's empirical observations about language are simple in themselves, their connection with their background is exceedingly complex. A careful exploration of controversial boundaries between factual discourse and other types of discourse would reveal some of the complexity. But even if the exploration is confined to factual statements, and a few other linguistic forms which are related to them, such as questions and commands, there is still a very complex connection between what Wittgenstein says and its background. Of course, the general idea of confusion between different areas of discourse is a simple one, however subtle and intricate the unravelling may be in particular cases. Even though the unravelling is elaborate, it might only be a matter of telling the complex truth to someone who has made a simple error. But what really complicates the relation between what Wittgenstein says and its background is the theory of deceptive pointing.

It may seem amazing that his later philosophy should get such a grip on people's minds, when what gives his factual observations their significance is something negative. The other has to be brought to see that his confusion does not point towards a genuine possibility, and that it does not even point to something outside the familiar areas of discourse which creates the impossibility. Is Wittgenstein's new philosophy then merely the removal of the débris of the philosophy of the past? If so, it would seem to be only of interest to specialists, and rather depressing for them.

His own remarks about his method often make this question more perplexing. He says, for instance, that the philosopher's treatment of a question is like the treatment of an illness. This suggests that it is only people's confusions that make philosophy necessary, and it then seems natural to take two further steps, and say that the confusions need never be made, and that only philosophers have made them. But what sort of illness did he have in mind? He repudiated the analogy with mental illness and the assimilation of his method to psychoanalysis, but probably not on the ground that there is nothing in this, but only on the ground that others had exaggerated it. There are, in fact, both points of resemblance and points of difference between his new method and psychoanalysis, but they need not be listed here. It is more important to ask whether he believed that the illness is confined to philosophers, or that complete prophylaxis was possible.

Are these confusions merely an occupational illness? First, it must be admitted that most of his remarks are placed against the background of confusions which have been made by philosophers. But then it is almost a tautology that those confusions were made by philosophers. For a person who had not reflected on the problems would not be in a position to make that kind of confusion, and a person who had reflected on them would already have made his entry into philosophy. A philosophical confusion is not like a solecism or a slip of the tongue, neither of which show that there has been any reflection on the things confused. Of course, a slip of the tongue may reveal something deeper, but, if it does, it will be something emotional, whereas the deep confusions of philosophy are confusions of the intellect and imagination, and, if any feelings lie behind them, they will usually be disinterested feelings, although this is not always so.

It would be a caricature of this view of philosophy to say that it represents that kind of confusion as an occupational illness. For what is being suggested is that, whereas an ordinary illness can be contracted at work and endured at home, this illness does not extend outside philosophy (and here 'philosophy' does not only mean 'academic philosophy'), and, more controversially, that this illness is an essential part of philosophy, and not a hazard. The idea is that philosophical remarks are fully intelligible only against the background of the confusions which are being treated, so that the confusions must be understood first, and that they cannot be understood unless their seductiveness is actually experienced. So when the other rehearses scenes from the past history of philosophy, this is not because Wittgenstein's philosophy is an exercise in criticism which needs a supply of other people's mistakes. The explanation is that whatever pushed the great problems of philosophy, such as necessity and the relation of mind to body, into the centre of the stage in the past, also makes them occupy the mind of any philosopher in the present.

But why should there not be complete prophylaxis against these confusions? Why should there not be a philosophy to end philosophy? Wittgenstein almost seems to have thought that this is what he had achieved when he completed the *Tractatus*. Would it not really be possible to achieve this result by the new method?

This is the important question. First, it must be realized that there is some irony in the comparison with an illness. The philosopher is driven by a passionate desire to understand the limits of language, and, when he tries to satisfy this desire, the first thing that inevitably happens is that his mind is filled with images which, though they are delusive, have a primitive naturalness which he must experience. Then, and only then, can he go on to achieve the understanding that he seeks. If he tries to go straight to the second stage without going through the first one he will suffer from what Wittgenstein calls 'loss of problems'. That really is a disease, unlike the first stage, which is a necessary torment, and only by an ironical half analogy a disease.

It is unfortunate that this half analogy was given such prominence by Wittgenstein. It would be better to think of his philosophy in a different way. In the *Tractatus* the limit of language was drawn with one great sweeping stroke, and he was evidently confident that it was a barrier which would be felt from the inside to be insurmountable. In his later work there has been a change of mind on both these points. He has come to think that the only way to understand the limit of language is to try to cross it and to return to language in its ordinary human setting only after a genuine, but of course necessarily unsuccessful attempt of this kind. So the limit is now to be plotted by a kind of oscillation, and not by a single well-defined movement. Incidentally, even this idea is to be found in the *Tractatus*.

These attempts to cross the limits of language have to be genuine, and it is known in advance that they will fail. There is no paradox here because the location of the limit is not known until the attempt has been made and it has failed. It would be impossible to take a Geiger counter beyond the limit of a uranium field without its ceasing to record radioactivity. But this does not mean that an attempt, which could be described in this way afterwards, could not seriously be made in order to plot the limit of the field.

Perhaps this way of looking at Wittgenstein's later philosophy shows what is wrong with the too literal reading of some of the things that he says about it. It would be absurd to expect complete prophylaxis, because, on his view of philosophy, that could be achieved only if people never even began to philosophize. When they philosophize the first stage cannot be left out. However, that in itself does not rule out the possibility of a philosophy to end philosophy. Why should there not be a book which dealt systematically and completely with every philosophical confusion?

Here all sorts of considerations come in. First, Wittgenstein always regarded philosophy as something personal. His hatred of academic philosophy has already been mentioned. What he felt was not that philosophy cannot be taught, but that, if the teaching of it is done by passing on philosophical results, it will merely be repetition and memorization without problems, and therefore without life. To be a philosopher is to philosophize, and the function of a philosophical book is to help people to philosophize for themselves. So even if one philosopher could finish the subject for himself, that would not mean that there was no philosophizing left for others to do.

However, it might mean that the best that the others could do would be to follow slowly and with much thought in the master's footsteps. But Wittgenstein certainly did not make any such claim for his own later work. It is highly improbable that such an achievement is even theoretically possible. Even if language were a fixed system, it is not certain that there would be no variation in philosophical reactions to it. Would there really be a fixed common stock of pictures from which the return journey to understanding would always begin? In any case, language is not a fixed system. Science, for example, has made enormous additions to it, and that kind of addition leads to internal rearrangement of what was already there.

Although it is not clear how much might conceivably be achieved along these lines, in his Preface to *Philosophical Investigations* Wittgenstein makes it quite clear what he thought of his own achievement. He regarded the book as a contribution to an indefinitely complex task, and he did not want it to spare other people the trouble of thinking but, if possible, to stimulate someone to thoughts of his own.

There is, as has been mentioned, something about his later method which is difficult to understand. Let us now revert to the difficulty. Suppose that it is granted that what gives philosophy its depth is always to be explained by the theory of deceptive pointing, and that the way in which linguistic boundaries always ought to be drawn is the way described by the theory of oscillation. Even if both these controversial theses are granted, it is not clear why the philosopher should altogether avoid theorizing. It is true that, granted those two theses, the work of presenting linguistic examples in philosophy will have a certain similarity with the work of an artist. The significance of the examples will be fully intelligible only to someone who has experienced the imagery which gives them their force. They must also be extremely carefully chosen, and there is an element of genius in some of Wittgenstein's choices. It is also understandable that he should be aware that it is risky to generalize, and that addiction to the habit is one of the things which explains why systematic philosophy is so often lifeless. A philosopher who was conscious of all this would naturally stress the individuality of the particular case, as in certain theories of art. But what is hard to understand is how Wittgenstein can have thought that examples from two different areas of discourse can ever be used in philosophy without implicit generalization about the differences between the two areas. Of course, a philosopher who seeks a simple overall pattern may well fail to find it, and then there would be some point in telling him that the only pattern is his own footprints in the dust. But if he has learned anything from his own exploration, will they not form minor patterns, governed by less sweeping generalizations?

The solution to this problem of interpretation might be that, when Wittgenstein disavowed theorizing, he only meant that he never tried to explain linguistic facts, but merely to present them. If this were all, he would only be rejecting theories which try to explain *a priori* necessities and impossibilities by finding some backing for them outside the relevant areas of discourse. His idea would then be that anyone who theorized in this way was deluded by the second of the two kinds of deceptive pointing which were distinguished earlier. There would be no suggestion that philosophy could proceed without any kind of implicit generalization about linguistic examples, and so the opposition between his later philosophy and systematic philosophy, though it would still exist, would not be so absolute.

This may be right. But there is reason to think that this is not the whole of the explanation of his opposition to theorizing, and that he went further than this. The question, how much further he may have gone, will be resumed later.

However that may be, the guarded hope which he expresses about his second book has certainly been fulfilled both by it and by his other later works. They immediately communicate his passionate desire to understand, and they communicate it to people to whom the problems, if they had been investigated in the old way, would have been, at least at first, inaccessible. They achieve this not because they are in any way dilutions or popularizations of philosophy, but because in him the sense of wonder took a special form. He saw the profound as an extra dimension of things which in themselves are very simple.

There are two final points which must be added to this account of Wittgenstein's later method. First, his treatment of the ownership of sensations, which is connected in an interesting way with his early ideas about Solipsism, goes far beyond the few jejune points which have been extracted from the example used here. But the purpose of this discussion has not been to introduce his doctrines, but only his method, by placing it on a bare stage. Secondly, no claim is being made that his later philosophy is merely an endless repetition of the dialectical drama which has just been put on that stage. Rather than say this, it would be better to say that he has no later method, because there would be some truth in that. But the truest account is that his dialectical plots are always variations and developments of these basic themes.

7 Necessity

Doctrine and method are intertwined in the second period of Wittgenstein's philosophy as they were in the first, but exposition has to start at some point. It was natural to begin the exposition of his early philosophy with doctrine rather than with method, because he was then philosophizing within the old conventions, and it is not so difficult to understand the general drift and setting of his remarks as it is to understand what they mean. In the later period this is reversed. As it becomes easier to understand what he says, it becomes more difficult to see the point of his saying it. This is why philosophers are often baffled by the later work, whereas non-philosophers are sometimes not sufficiently baffled by it. In neither period is it at all easy to follow his trains of thought. But in the later period it is the method that is puzzling, and that is why it has been taken first.

The mass of his later writings, some of them yet to be published, is prodigious. It is no good attempting to give even a summary of his main doctrines here. Instead, two of the most important ones will be selected for discussion, his account of necessity in this chapter, and of sensations in the following one. They are both connected with the shift towards anthropocentrism in his later philosophy. Incidentally, the discussion of them will provide a more complete picture of his method. The examples which have been used so far to illustrate his method may have achieved clarity at the cost of giving the false impression that it is easy to philosophize in the later style.

The abandonment of Z was an important stage in the

development of Wittgenstein's philosophy in the 1930s.[1] Z is the assumption that, whenever two propositions are logically related to one another, there will be within one of the two, or within both, some logical complexity which analysis could reveal. In the *Tractatus* he had used Z as one of the premisses of his elaborate proof of the thesis that all factual propositions are completely analysable into elementary propositions, which are logically independent of one another. This thesis put him in a position to extend his theory of necessary truth to cover every kind of case, except, of course, the necessary propositions of the system of the *Tractatus*. His theory was that all necessary truths are tautologies, or reducible by analysis to tautologies. The extension of this theory to provide a single uniform explanation of all necessary truth was possible only if all factual propositions really were completely analysable into elementary propositions. For only then could all sources of necessity be exhibited in the structure of language, so that there would be no sources of necessity which had to be left unanalysed in the natures of particular things. It is true that in the *Tractatus* the existence of tautologies presupposes that reality is composed of simple objects. But this is a general feature of reality, and the necessary truth, that it has this feature, belongs to the system of the *Tractatus*. What Wittgenstein thought that he had achieved was a single uniform explanation of all other necessary truths.

There always was an obvious difficulty in this extension of the theory of necessary truth. Though it could be seen to work for any range divided into two sections, each covered by a word which could be defined through the word covering the other, as is the case with the words 'crooked' and

1. See *Some Remarks on Logical Form*, Proceedings of the Aristotelian Society, Supplementary Vol. IX, 1929, pp. 162–71; and *Philosophische Bemerkungen*, ed. R. Rhees, Blackwell, 1964 (but written around 1930), pp. 105 ff and p. 317.

'straight', it could not be demonstrated that it worked for ranges divided into three or more sections, like the range of colours. For when there are three or more sections, it is implausible to suggest that the words can be defined through one another, for example, that 'yellow' can be defined as 'coloured, but neither red nor blue nor ... etc.; and even if such a definition were acceptable, it could hardly be regarded as one which revealed the internal complexity of the colour yellow. So it was difficult to see how the proposition, 'If a thing is yellow, it cannot be blue', could be reduced by analysis to a tautology.

Wittgenstein's reaction to this difficulty had been to claim that, although the theory could not be seen to work in this kind of case, it must work. All factual propositions, including those in which colours are mentioned, must be reducible to elementary propositions, even if nobody could see how the reduction was to be done. Because he relied on this general theory, he did not care much about the exact way in which the analysis would be carried out, and he was not much worried by his own inability to carry it out. However, later, when he reflected on the kind of thing that his general theory required, he began to see that it was unlikely that the requirement could ever be met. Suppose, for example, that necessary truths about colours were analysed into necessary truths about the velocities of particles. Then the difficulty would merely have been shifted to this lower level of analysis, because there would be a wide range of different velocities, which, without further analysis, would not yield to the treatment which the theory required. There are, of course, other ways in which colours might be analysed, but it looked as if any analysis, however far it was carried, would run up against the same difficulty. If this really was the case, the difficulty was insuperable, and the theory would have to be changed.

So he changed the theory, and allowed that elementary propositions are logically related to one another, and that colour propositions are elementary. In the *Tractatus*, he had said that a proposition is like a ruler laid against reality to measure it. But if a thing turned out to have one length when it was measured, it could not have any of the other lengths marked on the ruler. So his new view was that elementary propositions, such as those which mention colours, are like the intervals marked on a ruler, and that it is the whole system of these propositions which is like the ruler. So we do not apply elementary propositions to reality singly, but in systematically related groups. This was a step away from atomism and towards holism.

At the time Wittgenstein did not regard this change as a fundamental one. For he still adhered to the theory of elementary propositions, albeit in a new version, which as a matter of fact was very like the version which Russell proposed in 1918.[2] But the change can be seen as the beginning of something much bigger. For instead of making deductions from his essentialist theory of language, Wittgenstein had looked again at the empirical facts about language, and this was the beginning of the revolution which turned his philosophical method through one hundred and eighty degrees.

The change is also an interesting stage in the development of his doctrines. In the *Tractatus* all necessary truths except those of the system itself are either tautologies or reducible to tautologies. None of them are substantial necessary truths. Now a philosopher who holds this theory of necessary truth is likely to think that, if the theory had to be restricted in its scope because there were cases which it did not fit, that would show that in these cases the necessity had some independent backing outside the relevant area of discourse. His idea would be that, if a particular

2. 'The Philosophy of Logical Atomism', *Monist*, 1918–1919, reprinted separately by the University of Minnesota Press, and reprinted in *Logic and Knowledge*, ed. R. C. Marsh, Allen and Unwin, 1956.

necessary truth could not be taken home and dismantled behind the closed doors of language, that would be because it depended on something outside language in the nature of the things themselves. If he really were prepared to make this inference, he would be ready to adopt Realism rather than Nominalism if the argument went against him. He would suppose that, if it turned out that the scope of his theory of necessary truth had to be restricted, he would have to conclude that there is an objective connection between universals which pre-existed the formation of any language. In the example used, he would be forced to conclude that there is an objectively necessary connection between the two colours, yellow and blue. He would have to admit that they are objectively incompatible, and that their incompatibility is a feature of the system of colours which is not created by language, but discovered, and then incorporated in any viable system of colour words.

The interesting thing is that, when Wittgenstein changed his early theory of elementary propositions, he did not draw this conclusion. He might have been expected to draw it, because the *Tractatus* already contained the very general substantial necessary truth, that reality consists of simple objects. So why should he not now add specific substantial necessary truths about colours? And if such truths about colours were to be added, why not about other things too? In this way the objective structure of reality would become much more intricate. Even if, as seems probable, he did not distinguish between reality in so far as it can be caught in the network of any language and reality without this qualification, this objective structure of reality would still pre-exist the formation of any actual language. Any language which human beings devised would have to be connected up with this pre-existing structure, but, whereas in the *Tractatus* the points of connection had been few and general, they would now be many and specific.

But when Wittgenstein changed his early theory of elementary propositions, he did not draw this conclusion. His explanation of the necessary truth that, if a thing is yellow it cannot be blue, was nominalistic. According to him, it simply depends on the logical grammar of the two colour words. The way in which our language divides up the range of colours is not the only possible way, but, when it is done in this way, that necessary truth is automatically written into the rules for the use of our colour words. So someone who suggests that the rule be changed must be suggesting that we divide up the range in a different way. It is no objection to this view to point out that the rule cannot be used to reduce the necessary truth to a tautology. For it is merely an essentialist prejudice to suppose that there is only one way in which the necessary truth could depend on the logical grammar of the two colour words, and that that is the way which is described in the theory of the *Tractatus*. Why should their logical grammar not include features of their use which cannot be exhibited in analytical definitions, but which require us to look out through the windows of language at its application to selected things?

But it is more likely that the objection to Wittgenstein's explanation of this necessary truth would come from a different quarter. A Realist would claim that there must already be an objective connection between the two colours, even if he cannot state it without using our colour vocabulary. But Wittgenstein would treat this as a case of deceptive pointing. If the necessary truth seems to point beyond itself to its own backing in reality, we should not be deceived. There is nothing here except the fact that we ourselves have carved up the range of colours in a certain way. It is true that everything is what it is and not another thing, but this only means that there are indefinitely many distinctions which could be drawn in language, and the Realist evidently wants to claim more than this. It is also true that some ways of dividing up the range of colours are more natural than others. But again this does not help the

Realist, because any way of dividing it up, even an un-
natural way, will generate its own logical grammar. The
sources of necessity never lie outside the relevant areas of
discourse, and our desire for an objective backing, however
natural it may be, can never be satisfied. The only relevant
facts are facts about our linguistic practices. If the Realist
says that this leaves these practices floating in a void, that is
the right description of the situation from his point of view,
but then this point of view is his only because he has
already taken his stand on the assumption that necessary
truths ought to have a backing outside the relevant areas of
discourse.

If this is convincing, the reason is not that what the Realist says is actually false, but, rather, that what he says cannot be meant in the way in which he wants to mean it. It is
true that the two colours are incompatible, but, according
to Wittgenstein's view of the matter, this can only be
meant as an alternative way of expressing the Nominalist's
point, and not as an allusion to something independent backing up the logical grammar of the words. In a certain sense,
there can only be one theory here, or, as Wittgenstein
would put it, there cannot be any theory, but only a description of the linguistic facts. But perhaps the best way to
put it is that the only possible theory is the theory that
there are only the linguistic facts.

It is necessary to remember this point when we turn to
Wittgenstein's new theory of logical necessity, which he
began to develop in 1929, perhaps as a result of listening to
lectures by Brouwer.[3] For this theory is an application of
the same anthropocentric treatment to the truths of logic
and mathematics. The idea is that they too are simply based
on certain linguistic practices, and that any suggestion that

3. See G. H. von Wright: *Biographical Sketch*, pp. 12–13. Brouwer's
views on mathematical necessity certainly influenced Wittgenstein,
and may have given him the original impetus which got him moving
towards the generalized anthropocentrism of his later philosophy.

they have an independent objective backing is an illusion.
Now Wittgenstein's later philosophy often produces a sort
of intellectual vertigo, rather like the feeling that some
people get in aeroplanes, that there ought to be something
more than air beneath their feet; and, understandably, this
vertigo is felt more strongly at this point than at any other.
So it is important to remember that, rightly or wrongly,
Wittgenstein did not think that he was denying anything
that can be given a clear meaning. He believed that this was
yet another case, in fact the most spectacular case, of deceptive pointing. According to him, if logical and mathematical necessity appear to have some independent objective backing, that is merely an illusory projection of the
relevant linguistic practices. But it is hard to be sure
whether he is right, or even to be sure how to set about
answering the question whether he is right. Starting out on
a well-trodden path in the philosophy of mathematics, he
had pushed on relentlessly until he reached an uncharted
area, and he did not revise his notes for publication.[4] Con-
sequently both the subject itself and the interpretation of
what he says about it are extremely difficult.

How much had to be subtracted from the early theory of
logical necessity in order to arrive at the new theory? First,
of course, the ontology had to be taken away. But that was
done for a different reason. The theory of the *Tractatus* was
that the existence of truths of logic reveals that reality is
composed of simple objects. But that theory depended on
certain essentialist axioms and assumptions which were
abandoned later, and their abandonment left the status of
logical truths unaffected. In order to arrive at the new
theory, the old view of their status had to be changed. They
had to be given the sort of anthropocentric basis which in

4. They were published posthumously under the title *Remarks
on the Foundations of Mathematics* with an English translation by
G. E. M. Anscombe, ed. G. H. von Wright, R. Rhees and G. E. M.
Anscombe, Blackwell, 1956.

the *Tractatus* had been given to everything else, but not to them.

But what is the meaning of the suggestion that the truths of logic and mathematics have an anthropocentric basis? As soon as we try to understand its meaning we find ourselves in a world of vertiginous paradox. Does it really mean that logic and arithmetic developed out of certain choices made by the human race? If so, what could the other options possibly have been? Perhaps the first point which needs to be made here is that if these choices, if indeed there were any choices, were revoked, the results would be more far-reaching than they would be in the case of our colour vocabulary. For we could change the way in which we now divide up the range of colours without any big repercussions elsewhere. But there are many applications of mathematics, and logic pervades the whole of human thought. Suppose, for example, that we ceased to apply logical theorems in what we now regard as the correct impartial way: we might say, perhaps, that the theorem 'If p, and if if p then q, then q' should no longer be treated as something which could never be false. Or, to take an example from arithmetic, we might take the same view about the equation '$7 + 5 = 12$'. We would cancel the earlier general ratifications of these formulae, if indeed there were any ratifications of them, on the ground that they went too far. It is obvious that these cancellations would produce widespread chaos, unless perhaps the innovations could be regularized in some way. Someone might propose, for instance, that the arithmetical equation should be allowed to be false when it is applied to the particles of physics, on the ground that this would enable physicists to construct simpler laws, and perhaps he would support this by citing Einstein's treatment of geometry as a branch of physics.

But such regularizations would not satisfy the Realist. He would reject the whole idea that in logic and mathematics there are different choices which might set different standards of correctness. According to him, for each of these formulae there is something in the reality explored by logicians and mathematicians which makes it true, or there is something which makes it false. In the case of '$7+5=12$' there is something which makes it true, and so anyone who chose to allow that, when it is applied in certain areas, it may be false, would simply be choosing to make a mistake. The best way to establish this would be to offer him a proof of the equation. For if he gave the usual meaning to the terms used in the proof, he could not refuse to accept it, and so he would realize that what had seemed to him to be a choice which set a new standard of correctness was really and objectively a mistake.

This sounds like a strong position. How could Wittgenstein attack it without absurdity? Is he not driven back to a theory like that of the *Tractatus*? Of course, the old ontology has gone, but is he not forced to reaffirm the general thesis that the truths of logic and mathematics are a rigid pre-existing framework to which any language must connect itself, even if there are various options about the exact way in which the connections are to be made?

But, surprisingly, Wittgenstein does deny the Realist's point. He maintains that acceptance of any proof is an act of ratification which is independent of any previous acts of ratification. Nothing that we have done in the past forces us to ratify, or to withhold ratification from the proof which we are now being offered. This sounds absurd, because we naturally assume that the meanings of the terms used in the proof of the would-be theorem or equation must have been fixed in advance. But what Wittgenstein is suggesting is that their meanings were not completely fixed in advance, and that their full meanings accrue to them bit by bit when the later ratifications are made or withheld. This may be an amazing suggestion, but it is not incoherent.

However, almost everyone would find it more natural to follow the Realist's line here, and to say that, if anyone refused to ratify '$7+5=12$', that would show that he must be changing the meanings of the terms used in the proof of this equation, and not merely developing them in one of the ways which had always been left open. It is true that, when a rule of inference is first formulated, it does not contain within itself instructions for all its possible future applications. How could it? Nevertheless, it can be formulated in such a way that anyone who refused to apply it in what we would regard as the same way in the disputed proof would seem to be insanely perverse. He, of course, would say that he was applying it in the same way, because his criterion of sameness differed from ours. But to us this would sound like a bad joke.

It is interesting to observe that something very like this part of the controversy, yet not exactly like it, might have occurred in the argument about the colours. Suppose that someone, who had been taught the two colours, yellow and blue, by being shown examples, then applied them both to some muddy mixture, and claimed that he was using the words in the same way as his teacher. It is possible that this would be cleared up very quickly. The teacher could claim that the necessary truth 'If a thing is yellow it cannot be blue' was implicit in his original instruction by examples, and this would be a plausible claim if the instruction in the application of the word 'yellow' had included, as it ought to have done, examples of things which were not yellow, and the pupil might agree. So far, of course, this is not like the other controversy. Moreover, there is nothing here which is exactly like it. For there is no question of proving the necessary truth that, if a thing is yellow it cannot be blue. After the argument with the teacher the pupil can only ratify it directly, or refuse to ratify it directly. However, if in the other controversy it is possible to argue that a rule of inference might be given what we would call 'different interpretations' in different proofs without inconsistency, then it would be possible to argue here that something which had been directly ratified might be given what we would call 'different interpretations' in different contexts without inconsistency. After all, who is to say what counts as 'the same again'? So the pupil could treat the statement, that if a thing is yellow it cannot be blue, in this way, and refuse to apply it to flames, or some such thing, and the teacher could only say that he must be insane.

This raises the question, whether the word 'ratification' has any clear meaning in the theory of necessary truth which Wittgenstein seems to be offering. But it was always obvious that this would come into question. For the kind of solvent which he applies to necessary truths which are being used as rules of inference in suggested proofs can obviously be applied to all necessary truths, including those which have just been directly ratified. So it seems that, if Wittgenstein's theory were right, all communication would break down.

But at this point we have to be very careful how we interpret his whole enterprise. In his later philosophy it is always easier to understand what he is saying than it is to understand the point of his saying it, and this is conspicuously the case here. So it is important to remember that he, at least, did not think that he was denying anything that could be given a clear meaning. He was trying to demonstrate not that logic and mathematics do not rest on a Realistic basis, but only that that basis cannot provide any independent support for them. To put the point in the terms introduced earlier, the sources of the necessities of logic and mathematics lie within those areas of discourse, in actual linguistic practices, and, when those necessities seem to point to some backing outside the practices, the pointing is deceptive, and the idea that the backing is independent is an illusion. If this is right, then what the Realist says cannot be meant in the way in which he wants to mean it, and there can only be one theory here, the theory that there are only the facts. If this conclusion sounds sceptical, it will only be to the Realist that it sounds sceptical. For, of course, Wittgenstein was not offering a theory designed to show that logic and mathematics, which everyone felt to be so safe, in fact the safest things of all, are really in a precarious position. The question is, granted that they are safe, what makes them safe, and we cannot say that Wittgenstein's answer to this question is inadequate, when the standard of adequacy is fixed by a rival theory which he does not even regard as an intelligible alternative.

If this really is the drift of Wittgenstein's remarks, how are we to explain the vertiginous paradoxes? And is what he says convincing? There is one important fact which has not yet been explicitly mentioned, and which might put us in a position to answer these two questions. The fact is that, if logical and mathematical truths are ratified, there is no viable alternative to ratifying them. It is true that geometry may be treated as a branch of physics, but it is not true that this shows that proofs are given and refused ratification entirely independently of one another in the way that Wittgenstein envisages. So here is a second conspicuous difference between this case and the case of the colours.

Perhaps this puts us in a position to explain Wittgenstein's paradoxes. He is not suggesting that, if someone refused ratification to the formula 'If p, and if if p then q, then q', and to other useful formulae of this kind, and claimed that by his criteria he was still using the terms in the same way, he could still go on thinking and speaking effectively. His point is only that it is a contingent fact that human beings agree in their ratifications, however hopeless the situation would be if they did not agree, and that this agreement is the foundation of logic and mathematics.

But is this convincing? Suppose that the Realist claimed that the reason why there is no viable alternative to 'ratifying' the truths of logic and mathematics is simply that it would be a mistake to reject them, and that this shows that the idea that they depend on 'ratification' is an error. In reply, Wittgenstein would probably make four points. First, automatic and unhesitating ratification is still ratification. Secondly, the non-viability of the alternative is solely a matter of its consequences, and has nothing to do with incorrectness. But thirdly, when we judge deviant systems of non-ratification by our standards of correctness, and reach the inevitable verdict that they are mistaken, we must realize that this judgement can be reciprocated, and that it does nothing to show that our system has any independent backing. So fourthly, it is only a contingent fact that there is as much agreement in these ratifications as there is, and it is on this fact alone that logic and mathematics depend.

If it is difficult to see which side is right, it may at least be a little clearer what Wittgenstein is trying to do, and why it is difficult to see which side is right. He wants to show that there is only one possible theory here, and that is the anthropocentric theory, and that there is no way of formulating Realism as a genuinely different theory about an independent objective backing. He would prefer to put this by saying that there cannot be any theory here, but only a description of the linguistic facts. Perhaps it would be an acceptable compromise to say that the only possible theory is the theory that there are only the linguistic facts.

But the difficulty is that there are two ways of interpreting the fact that there is no viable alternative to so-called 'ratification'. Wittgenstein would interpret it pragmatically: the alternative would have disastrous consequences. But may it not be that it would have disastrous consequences only because, as the Realist claims, it would be mistaken? Why should the Realist not turn the tables on Wittgenstein, and claim that his theory gives the true basis of logical and mathematical necessity, and that Wittgenstein's theory cannot be formulated as a genuinely distinct rival? For actual linguistic practices are relevant only when they accord with pre-existing necessities. It is not that we project our ideas into a void, but, rather, that there is something there which, if we are fortunate, will be mapped on to our ideas.

But, Wittgenstein could object that the Realist is failing to see the force of the third of his four points: any system of ratifications will have its own standard of correctness, and, when it judges other systems by its own standard, the verdict will be that they are mistaken: and any system will claim to have an independent objective backing, which, according to its view, the others do not have. So—but perhaps the discussion may be left at this point.

8   Sensations

The second doctrine to be discussed is concerned with the language in which we express and describe our sensations. According to Wittgenstein, this language is not, and cannot be private. When he says this, he means that it is not, and cannot be necessarily unteachable. An empirical examination of it shows that it is not private in this sense, and an argument, which is based ultimately on certain empirical facts about the meaning of the word 'language', shows that it cannot be private in this sense.

It may seem odd that he should find it necessary to argue for both these points. For is it not obvious that our language for sensations is in fact taught and passed down from generation to generation? And is that not more than enough to show that it is not necessarily unteachable? And once that has been established, what is the point of asking the further question whether it could have been necessarily unteachable?

But it must be recognized that he is not arguing against someone who doubts that this part of our language is in fact taught, or is, at least, what we call 'taught'. He is arguing against a philosophical theory from which, according to him, it would follow that it could not be, and therefore was not taught. Let us for the moment call this theory 'C' and leave its specification until later. Someone who held C would either completely deny that the consequence, which, according to Wittgenstein, follows from it, really does follow from it; or else, he would allow that there is something about sensations, which, given the truth of C, could not be communicated, but he would claim that this only shows how true C is, because in fact that element never is com-

municated, and he would then make the further claim that
what ordinarily counts as teaching this part of our language
is perfectly compatible with C. Against this, Wittgenstein is
arguing that, if C were correct, this part of our language
would be necessarily unteachable, and therefore it would be
an illusion that it was in fact taught.

This part of the controversy has the same structure as the
earlier discussion of Hume's theory of sensations. Hume
treated sensations as if their criterion of identity were
exactly like the criterion of identity of material objects. But
of course he did not think that there really was an answer
to the question 'Where was B's sensation before he had it?'
any more than Wittgenstein's adversary would think that
the language in which we express and describe our sensations is not, in fact, taught, or at least what we call 'taught'.
In both cases the absurdity is alleged to be the consequence
of a philosophical theory, and the proponent of the theory
denies the allegation. But the difficult thing for him is to
make good his denial by showing that the alleged consequence really does not follow from his theory.

It would be an understatement to say that there is an
analogy between C and Hume's theory of sensations. For C
may be characterized in a hostile way as the theory that
sensations are more like material objects than in fact they
are, and Hume's theory actually is an example of a theory
which exaggerates the similarity between these two kinds
of thing. However, this indefinite characterization of C
obviously will not do. Wittgenstein's general idea may be
clear enough: if the assimilation of sensations to material
objects is taken too far, each person's sensations will be
completely inaccessible to everyone else, and so this part
of our language will become necessarily unteachable. But
at what point does the assimilation begin to be excessive?
What is needed here is a detailed list of similarities and
differences. In fact, we have come back to the point
reached in the earlier discussion. Discourse about sensations

and discourse about material objects are allegedly confused, and the confusion seems to point beyond the relevant logical space to the new possibility that our language for sensations might continue to exist, even if it were removed from its present setting in the rest of our language. But this pointing is deceptive, and the way to dispel the illusion is to take the other slowly and carefully along the line which divides the two areas.

But, as usual, something else is needed in addition to the demonstration that there has been a confusion. It is also necessary to examine the supposed new possibility, towards which, according to Wittgenstein, the confusion points, and to demonstrate that it is not a genuine possibility. This is why he goes on to argue for his second thesis, that there could not be a necessarily unteachable language. His argument is that, if his adversary were right, our language for sensation could have existed outside its present human setting of stimulus and response. Now stimulus and response are described in our language for material objects. So, according to Wittgenstein, if the other were right, our language for sensations could have existed outside its present setting alongside our language for material objects. In that case it would be necessarily unteachable even by his adversary's standards of teaching. But, Wittgenstein argues, this uprooting of our language for sensations, which would make it necessarily unteachable, would also prevent it from being a language, given the empirical facts about the meaning of the word 'language'. The details of this argument will be expounded later. At the moment what is being explained is only Wittgenstein's strategy, and the reason why he found it necessary to establish his second thesis.

This topic is less difficult than the previous one, and Wittgenstein's treatment of it is full, and evidently revised by him before publication in *Philosophical Investigations*. It is, therefore, surprising to find that there has been a wide divergence of opinion not only about the topic itself, but also about the interpretation of his treatment of it. This is partly because he does not sufficiently distinguish between the different versions of his adversary's thesis. But it is also because the whole area is so well trodden that it is easy to make the mistake of ascribing to Wittgenstein some familiar line of thought which in fact he is not following. The discussion in this chapter will only be designed to isolate some of the main issues in this arena, and not to settle them. It will suffice if they can be presented separately outside the cloud of dust which is nearly always raised when they are all put together.

First, something needs to be said about the importance of this topic and its place in the history of philosophy. The previous discussion was concerned with the foundations of logic and mathematics. This one is concerned with the foundations of factual knowledge, considered from an epistemological point of view rather than from the logical point of view adopted in the *Tractatus*. Now the question, where these foundations lie, has been answered by philosophers in many different ways. Some say that the basic propositions are about material objects, and others say that they are about sensations, or about sense-data, because the word 'sensation' may have too narrow a use to perform such a general service. It is also possible to take the view that they do not have to be about any single type of thing, so that there are no foundations in that sense, and the metaphor is misleading. In the pre-linguistic period of philosophy these views, or at least the first two of them, were expressed in other ways. For example, Berkeley held that the immediate objects of knowledge are 'ideas of perception', or, as we might say, sense-data, and it is amazing how natural he found it to transfer the properties of material objects to these sense-data. His theory is a perfect example of C.

It has already been mentioned that Wittgenstein did not identify the elementary propositions of the *Tractatus* with sense-datum propositions, or with any other type of proposition characterized by its subject matter. But he suggested this identification, among others, in the *Notebooks*, and in the work that he did about 1930 he was prepared to consider that sense-datum propositions might be basic. So his new doctrine is a rejection of a theory which in the past he certainly had not found absurd. But this is comparatively unimportant. What is more important is that the rejected theory had been, in one form or another, the dominant theory of perception since the time of Descartes. Of course it would be a mistake to assume that all versions of this theory of perception inevitably involve the exaggerated assimilation which is the mark of C. But, arguably, many of them did involve it.

In the development of Wittgenstein's own philosophy the new doctrine gets its importance from a different quarter. First, it must be observed that the arguments which he uses in support of it are directed not only against theories which take the assimilation of sensations to material objects too far, but also against theories which treat emotions, desires or intentions in this way. The doctrine is really a general one. Public criteria are needed across the whole range of mental phenomena, and so the language of mental phenomena could not exist in isolation. Only a self-contained language can exist in isolation. But the language of mental phenomena is not self-contained, and if it appears to be, this is only because it has been excessively assimilated to the language of physical phenomena, which really is self-contained, and does not rest on a further auxiliary language.

Another point which ought to be made in this connection is that the concept of an intention ought to stand at, or near, the centre of any theory of meaning, and yet it is not even mentioned in the theory of meaning of the *Tractatus*. It is not mentioned there, because, at a certain stage in the development of his theory of elementary propositions, Wittgenstein stopped when he might have gone on. He stopped at the correlation of words with objects. The result is that his early theory of meaning is a sort of abstract projection of human linguistic practices. If he had gone on to ask how these correlations could be made, he would have said more about people, and their intentions, and the rules that are associated with their intentions. A word is not brought to life by mere juxtaposition with the thing which it designates. Any attempt to say what more is needed inevitably brings in the philosophy of mind, which scarcely makes an appearance in the lunar landscape of the *Tractatus*.

Putting these two points together, we may say that in the development of Wittgenstein's philosophy the new doctrine gets its importance from its contribution to the later theory of meaning. Meaning is linked with intention, and intention is linked with public criteria. It follows that, though the later philosophy is anthropocentric, it could never be solipsistic. The base line to which we must always return is a shared language with public criteria. Naturally, this does not rule out the language for sensations. But it does rule out any interpretation of that language which would cut it off from the shared base line.

In the discussion which follows there are four points which must be kept in mind. First, when the word 'private' qualifies language, it always means 'necessarily unteachable'. Secondly, Wittgenstein needs to specify the points at which C exaggerates the similarity between sensations and material objects. Then he has to demonstrate that, if C, as specified, were true, our language for sensations would be necessarily unteachable. Finally, he must demonstrate that C really does point to the supposed possibility that this part of our language could have existed outside its present setting, and that this is not a genuine possibility.

Let us begin with a non-controversial point. Our language for sensations is teachable only because it has many links with the language for material objects. Without these links, it would be necessarily unteachable. As an example, Wittgenstein observes that a human being in pain will behave in various characteristic ways, and so the word 'pain' is linked to the description of this behaviour, which, of course, belongs to the language for material objects. This link can be used to teach a child in pain to use the word 'pain'. Of course, the child does not have to be able to describe its own behaviour or even be aware of it, but the teacher recognizes it as the natural expression of pain, and he replaces it with the word, which is an artificial expression of pain.

Wittgenstein does not say that this is the only kind of link which can be used in this way. It is obvious that the link with the description of the stimulus is at least equally important, and that some of the discriminations which we make between sensations could not be linked with distinctive natural reactions because there are none. For example, although a child's natural tendency to hold the part of the body where the pain is felt is one of the bases of the language for locating sensations, it cannot be the only one : for it does not make an adequate distinction between surface and interior, and for this distinction, and for some of the more precise interior locations we have to rely on stimulus. There are also other kinds of link which can be used in teaching the language for sensations. For example, the sensation which immediately precedes a yawn is not expressed by a yawn, and there are analogical descriptions of sensations, like 'pins and needles'.

So there are several varieties of what might be called 'teaching links', and an adequate discussion of them would have to include a description of the ways in which the pupil fills in the gaps, and makes moves which go beyond his literal instructions. It would be absurd to suppose that the teacher would need to link every conceivable proposition about a sensation with its own proposition about a material phenomenon, in order to complete the course of instruction, and that the pupil never did anything for himself. In fact, if the pupil were merely a passive recipient of information, there are parts of the language for sensations which he would never learn. Analogical descriptions provide an example of the kind of thing which only the pupil can do for himself; in other cases, such as the transference of the concept of intensity from one field of sensations to another, his contribution may not be indispensable, but it certainly speeds up the process of learning.

It is necessary to emphasize the variety of teaching links, because Wittgenstein shows a tendency, unusual in him, to concentrate too exclusively on the word 'pain' and its link with the natural expressions of pain, and, as a result, he treats what are really descriptions of sensations as if they were verbal expressions of sensations. However, this aspect of his new doctrine will be ignored. Also, the complications which are brought in by the different lateral moves which the pupil can make for himself will be left out. For Wittgenstein's first point is simple and valid; a language for sensations without teaching links would be necessarily unteachable, and then there is the question, whether it would be a language at all.

This point is evidently not enough in itself to enable Wittgenstein to complete the first half of his case. For the first of the two things which he had to demonstrate was that, if C were true, our language for sensations would be necessarily unteachable, and all that has been established so far is that a language for sensations without teaching links would be necessarily unteachable.

However, we now have one of the steps in his demonstration: if our language for sensations had no teaching links, it would be necessarily unteachable. The other step which he has to take is to show that, if C were true, our language for sensations would have no teaching links. But how exactly is C to be specified? This question cannot be postponed any longer.

C is the theory which treats sensations as if they were

more like material objects than in fact they are. But what is the specific point at which the assimilation becomes excessive, and by becoming excessive severs the teaching links of this part of our language? This is the crucial question, and it is here that the debate begins to get more difficult.

Wittgenstein's answer to this question is in two parts. First, he specifies C as the theory which says that a child under instruction can establish the meaning of the word 'pain' for himself by turning his attention inwards onto the right kind of sensation, and affixing the word to it. Here the idea behind the theory is that what the child does is exactly like what he does when he establishes the meaning of the word 'rose' for himself by turning his attention outwards on to the right kind of flower, and affixing the word to it. It is, of course, the teacher who tells him when he is in fact having the right kind of sensation, or is looking at the right kind of flower. Secondly, Wittgenstein specifies C as the theory which says that a person who has a sensation, such as a pain, may know that he has it. This, of course, suggests that there is also the possibility that he might not be sure that he had it, in spite of knowing the meaning of the word 'pain'. Here the idea behind the theory is that the phrase 'I know that' may be prefixed to the proposition 'I am in pain' in exactly the same way that it may be prefixed to the proposition 'This is a rose'. It can be prefixed to the latter proposition precisely because there really is also the possibility that he might not be sure that it was one, and might be mistaken, although he knew the criteria for roses, a possibility which would be realized if, for example, the light were bad.

These two points are not confined to the concept of pain. Quite generally, C assimilates sensations to material objects in two ways, both of them, according to Wittgenstein, mistaken. It says that a word for a type of sensation gets its meaning by being correlated with a sensation of that type, just like a word for a type of material object; and it says

that a person who has a sensation may be mistaken in his
verbal reaction to it, and not merely untruthful, just as he
may be mistaken in his description of a material object.

It is not entirely clear how these two specifications of C
are supposed to be related to one another. If the affixing of
a word to a sensation were exactly like the affixing of a
word to a material object, then it would be possible to be
mistaken in one's verbal reaction to one's own sensation in
spite of knowing the meaning of the word used. But perhaps this is to read too much into the phrase 'exactly like'.
For when Wittgenstein offers the first specification of C, he
is trying to isolate the suggestion that the meaning of a
sensation word is learned ostensively in the privacy of the
mind, and he is not concerned with what the pupil does
later after he has graduated. So probably the two specifications give two independent axioms which, taken together,
constitute the theory C. Anyway, Wittgenstein argues that
it is a consequence of the first axiom that a person could
never know what sensation another was having, and that a
further consequence of this is that our language for sensations would be necessarily unteachable. His adversary
denies these contentions. Wittgenstein's reason for rejecting
the second axiom will be given later.

At this point it might help to recall the much less intricate discussion of Hume's theory of sensations. Hume
would not have accepted the absurd implication that there
is an answer to the question, where B's sensation was before
he had it. But he found it difficult to cut this implication out
of his theory.[1] Similarly, Wittgenstein's adversary would
not accept the implications which Wittgenstein finds in his
theory, and, however difficult the task may be, he must
show that it does not really have those implications. Just as
Hume cannot take shelter in the fact that there is no answer
to that question, so too Wittgenstein's adversary cannot

1. See *Treatise of Human Nature*, Bk. I, Part 4, Section v, and the
Appendix.

take shelter in the fact that our language for sensations is teachable. In both cases a philosophical theory about the facts is under attack, and it is no defence to point out that the alleged absurd consequences do not square with the facts. That is precisely the attacker's point. The defender has to show that the alleged consequences do not really follow from the theory. But how is he to do that?

The simplest way would be to claim that one person can argue by analogy from his own case to the cases of other people. If in his own case a certain type of sensation has certain teaching links, then it is probable that the same teaching links point to the same type of sensation in other people, and we rely on this probability when we learn and teach the language for sensations. Rightly or wrongly, Wittgenstein rejected the claim that this would count as teaching, on the ground that there would never be any possibility of establishing that the lesson had been given or taken successfully. Since this is a clear issue, it will not be pursued here.

A more subtle attempt to block Wittgenstein's inferences from C would be to claim that, although the pupil does correlate the word 'pain' with sensations of a certain type, there is a difference between what happens in this case and what happens when a word is correlated with a type of material object. For the word 'pain' simply means 'sensation of a type which has such and such teaching links'. So if, unknown to us, and perhaps unknowably to us, the same teaching links pointed to different kinds of sensation in different people, those differences would not be picked up in the meaning of the word 'pain'. They would be left on the plate untouched. Naturally, nothing quite like this can happen to words in the language for material objects. For that part of language is the base line for us, and it does not need teaching links with some further, auxiliary part of language.

Does this more subtle theory fit Wittgenstein's first specification of C? In one way it does, because it says that the pupil establishes the meaning of the word 'pain' for himself by turning his attention inwards onto the right kind of sensation and affixing the word to it, and so it is not surprising to find that Wittgenstein rejects this theory. But there is another feature of the theory which might lead us to say that it does not fit Wittgenstein's first specification of C: the word would not draw its meaning from the sensation in exactly the same way that a word for a type of material object draws its meaning from an example used in instruction. But, however we classify this theory, there is no doubt that it neatly avoids the absurdity of a theory like Berkeley's, which merely transfers the properties of material objects to sensations and goes on from there. It also gives an attractively flexible account of the meanings of sensation words: any differences which came to be detected between person and person could be dealt with in various ways after they had come to light, but before that they would merely be a matter for speculation, and, if they existed at all, they could not be taken up into the vocabulary for sensations, but would be inevitably left on the plate.

It would have been better if Wittgenstein's characterization of C had been more detailed, so that he could have distinguished between this subtle development of it and the straightforward version of it. Let us distinguish them here by calling the first 'C-subtle', and the second 'C-crude'. C-subtle was worked out by some of the philosophers of the Vienna Circle in the 1930s.[2] It has also been ascribed to Wittgenstein himself. This is a misinterpretation, but not an altogether surprising one, given the doubt about the question, what does count as a development of C for him. If he had adopted C-subtle, he would have avoided behaviourism without cutting off the language for sensations from its

2. E.g. by R. Carnap, *Philosophy and Logical Syntax*, Psyche Miniatures, Kegan Paul, 1935, p. 88 ff.

base line in the language for material objects, and this is certainly what he wanted to achieve. But in fact he did not adopt it, and he tried to achieve his aim in another way, which is not so easy to understand.

Some philosophers reject C-subtle on the ground that a full description of the teaching links would be endlessly complicated, and therefore could not give anything so definite as the meaning of a word for a type of sensation. But this was not Wittgenstein's reason for rejecting it. For any theory, which, like his, assigns public criteria to words for types of sensations, has to allow that that kind of complication, however great it may be, is an unavoidable feature of the meanings of the words. His reason for rejecting it is that it would give every sensation word a private meaning, or perhaps a private reference in addition to its public meaning.

But someone who wanted to defend C-subtle would claim that, though the connection between reference and meaning is close, it is not so close that, if the reference is private, the meaning must be private too. He would point out that everything depends on the way in which the private reference is made, and that in his theory it is made in a way which ensures that it does not contribute to the meaning of the phrase 'sensation of a type which has such and such teaching links', just as the actual reference of the phrase 'a person's favourite cocktail' does not contribute to its meaning. There is, of course, a big difference between the ways in which the two phrases are applied: for it is possible to find out which cocktail is a particular person's favourite, whereas it is always difficult, and sometimes impossible to find out how, if at all, sensations of the type specified vary from person to person. But the defender of C-subtle would claim that this difference does not upset the theory, because in the specification of the type of sensation the variable stands with promiscuously open, but never really embracing arms. What fills them in each person's case is a matter of indifference to the meaning of the phrase. All that C-subtle requires is that, if, unknown to us, sensations of pain did vary from person to person, at least they would have to remain constant for each particular person. For if they suddenly and completely changed their character for a particular person, he would become a baffling case, because he could always with perfect sincerity deny that he was in pain, in spite of the fact that all the public criteria for his being in pain, except, of course, his own verbal reactions, were fulfilled.

At this point it is not entirely clear how the debate goes on. There is a lacuna, because Wittgenstein does not elaborate his reasons for rejecting C-subtle. Perhaps he would argue that the defence which has just been sketched cannot be valid, because it allows that something, which we would not regard as a possibility, is a possibility. It allows that a person might always have had from birth the wrong kind of sensation correlated with the teaching links of pain. It is true that, if this were so, we would probably never discover that it was so, but that does not make it any easier for the defence. For according to the defence, it would still be a possibility, but in fact we would not regard it as a possibility.

It is not certain that this was Wittgenstein's reasoning. But if it was, his adversary would certainly reply that the objection is misdirected. It is all right to direct it against C-crude, which treats the naming of sensations exactly like the naming of material objects. C-crude really would allow the possibility that throughout a person's life there might be in his case a divorce between being in pain and satisfying the public criteria for being in pain. According to C-crude such a person would always have the wrong kind of sensation whenever he satisfied the public criteria of pain, and so he would not be in pain. But the phrase 'wrong kind of sensation' is not used in this way by C-subtle. In fact, the whole point of C-subtle is that, even if he did have what C-crude calls 'the wrong kind of sensation', it would not be the wrong kind of sensation, and we would not say that he was not in pain. On the contrary, we would say that he was in pain, whatever the precise further character of his sensations might be. That is the function of the variable.

The difficulty at this point in the debate is that there is a lack of clarity in Wittgenstein's position. He certainly mentions and rejects C-subtle. But his reason for rejecting it seems to be a valid reason only for rejecting C-crude. So perhaps he believed that any theory which brings in an inner reference to a particular type of sensation in each person's case will inevitably treat this inner reference as the dominant factor in the meaning of the sensation word. If this were inevitable, C-subtle would do it too. It is then a simple matter to argue that, if the inner reference is treated in this way, it will carry the word with it wherever it goes, and so the connection with the teaching links might be broken in every case. But is this a convincing objection to C-subtle? Why must it treat the inner reference in this way, as something which is a completely detachable and dominant factor in the meaning of the sensation word? This question will be left at this point, because, whatever the right answer to it may be, the issue has now been sufficiently isolated from the other issues in this area.

There are all sorts of new considerations which have so far been held back, but which might now be brought in. For instance, nothing has yet been said about physiology, or about neurological criteria. Is not this whole debate too narrowly confined to views about sensations which have their sources in introspective psychology and behaviourism? Of course, from the fact that so much of the material of the debate comes from these sources, it does not follow that what is being discussed is an empirical question of psychology. The question under discussion is, to what extent sensations are like material objects, and this is not a direct empirical question, like the question to what extent wasps are like ants. It is a question about the possibilities, or, as Wittgenstein put it in his earlier period, about the logical space of the language for sensations, or, as he often put it in his later period, about the logical grammar of sensation words. Certainly, he regarded it as a question to be answered by citing the relevant empirical facts about language. But it is not a direct empirical question about sensations. It, therefore, brings in introspective psychology and behaviourism only in an oblique way. But why should it not bring in neurology too in the same oblique way?

This suggestion will not be pursued here, in spite of its importance. For it would take us too far from the debate between Wittgenstein and his adversary. The next thing that is required here is an explanation of the transition to his second demonstration, that there could not be a necessarily unteachable language.

He is undoubtedly right in his assumption that, when C-crude bases the meaning of a sensation word on inner references to sensations of a particular type, it will make these inner references completely detachable and dominant in the way already explained. If he had simply restricted his attack to C-crude, his position would have been clear and convincing. But he also mentions C-subtle, and rejects it for the same reason. This part of his strategy is obscure. One thing, however, is clear : he believes that anyone who does make the inner reference completely detachable and dominant is automatically committed to the thesis that there might be a necessarily unteachable language, and he wants to demonstrate that this is not a real possibility.

One reason why he moves on to his second demonstration, that there could not be a necessarily unteachable language, is that he feels it necessary to drag this alleged possibility out into the open in order to destroy it. He thinks that, when the discussion centres on our language for sensations, the new and exciting possibility, if indeed it is one, can hide in the shelter of the fact that this part of our language actually does have teaching links. Of course, he can argue, as he has been arguing so far in this exposition, that, if C were true, these teaching links would be quite ineffective. But, if this is right, a clearer way of focusing onto the consequences of C would be to give up the discussion of this part of our language, and to describe a language which merely satisfied the specifications of C without all the paraphernalia of arguably unusable teaching links. It is important to observe that this transition is legitimate only if the inner reference really is treated by his adversary as something which is completely detachable and dominant.

All this can be put in the terminology which was introduced earlier. C confuses discourse about sensations with discourse about material objects. This confusion seems to point to the new and exciting possibility that there might be a necessarily unteachable language. But this pointing is deceptive, because it can be demonstrated that a necessarily unteachable language is not a real possibility. It is important for Wittgenstein to argue against the pure form of the suggestion that it is a possibility, partly for the reason already given, and partly for another reason. Someone might accept his first demonstration, that, if C were true, our language for sensations would be necessarily unteachable, but he might maintain that this does not refute C, but only shows that, contrary to appearances, our language for sensations is not really teachable, and that we do not ever really communicate about such matters. So far it has been assumed that his adversary would concede that, if C represented this part of our language as necessarily unteachable, C must be false. But there is also another possibility : he might accept the inference, the conclusion and the premiss. However, this is a less important threat.

What has to be proved is that a necessarily unteachable language is not a real possibility. Wittgenstein's proof is simple. Our language for sensations would be necessarily unteachable if it were removed from its circle of teaching links. Now suppose that it were uprooted in this way, and that you were still trying to use it. There would be for any given statement that you might make only two possibilities: either you would be under the impression that it was true, or you would be under the impression that it was false. Neither of these two possibilities would subdivide into two further cases, the case in which your impression was correct, and the case in which your impression was incorrect. For since your statements would have been cut off from their teaching links, there would be no possible check on the correctness of your impressions. But it is an essential feature of any language that there should be effective rules which a person using the language can follow and know that he is following. Yet in the circumstances described there would be no difference between your being under the correct impression that you were following a rule and your being under the incorrect impression that you were following a rule, or, at least, there would be no detectable difference even for you. So there would be no effective rules in this so-called 'language'. Anything that you said would do. Therefore, it would not really be a language, and what prevented it from being a language would be the absence of teaching links, which, if they had been there, could have been used as checks. So what prevented it from being a language would be the thing that prevented it, indeed the only thing that could prevent it from being teachable. Therefore, there cannot be a necessarily unteachable language.

It is, at first sight, surprising that Wittgenstein should use this particular argument. For it seems to depend on the assumption that a person who knows the meaning of the word 'pain' might be mistaken, and not merely untruthful in his verbal reactions to his own pain. But this assumption is the second axiom of C. So it looks as if Wittgenstein is now borrowing this axiom from the very theory that he is attacking. But in fact there is no inconsistency in his strategy. The explanation is that our language for sensations is set in a circle of teaching links, and so, although, according to Wittgenstein, the person who has the sensation cannot be mistaken about it, that is only because he has already learned the meaning of the appropriate sensation word through the teaching links. These teaching links provide rules which are effective, and not mere sham rules. For in the early stages the teacher can actually use them to correct the pupil's mistakes. Later, when the pupil has graduated, the rules will still be available for him as a sort of safety net, but he will not need to use them, because he will find that he is unable to make mistakes in his verbal reactions to his own sensations. He can only be untruthful about them. So the only use that will be made of the rules at this stage will be made by other people, who will use them against him in order to discover when he is being untruthful. There is, therefore, no inconsistency in Wittgenstein's argument.

However, there is room for doubt about its precise interpretation. What exactly is meant by the supposition which Wittgenstein makes for the sake of the argument, the supposition that our language for sensations has been removed from its circle of teaching links? Is he supposing that it has been not only cut off from its teaching links, but also, quite generally, segregated from the language for material objects? *I.e.* is he supposing that the person who speaks this uprooted language for sensations does not know any part of the language for material objects? If so, it would be difficult, if not impossible, for his adversary to rebut the contention that this so-called 'language' would not be a language at all. For nothing that the speaker said could ever be checked. This is important. For many philosophers have claimed that the sense-datum language is basic in the natural sense of that word: it could stand alone as the foundation of all factual discourse, even if no superstructure were added to it. According to this version of Wittgenstein's argument, that would be impossible, because what those philosophers call 'superstructure' is in fact the most important part of the foundations.

Or is Wittgenstein supposing that our language for sensations has been removed from its circle of teaching links, but is spoken by someone who also knows some parts of the language for material objects? There is some evidence that this is what he is supposing. But in that case his adversary will be on stronger ground. For he can now argue that the speaker's memory can be checked when he makes statements about material objects, and then, having passed this test successfully, it can be used without any possibility of a check, but nevertheless with reasonable confidence of regular results, when he makes statements about his own sensations. Wittgenstein's adversary could not use this argument before, when it was supposed that the language for sensations was not only cut off from its own teaching links. but also entirely segregated from the language for material objects. But he can use it now that the speaker of the language for sensations is allowed some knowledge of the language for material objects. He will back it up with the charge that Wittgenstein has simply assumed that, if it is impossible to verify directly, whether the speaker's impression that he is following a rule for the use of a sensation word is correct or incorrect, then these are not two distinct possibilities. Is it not enough that there should be indirect confirmation drawn from the speaker's checkable statements about material objects? But is this really enough? At this point the general question of the validity of the verification principle is raised. Is the meaning of a statement the method of its verification, and is an unverifiable statement therefore meaningless? Is indirect confirmability not enough? Here this issue may be left.

The discussion now swings back to the question, what sort of account should be given of our language of sensations in its actual setting. If what Wittgenstein's adversary has just said is correct, then, even if the inner references were completely detachable and dominant, this part of our language would still be a genuine language. However, he would still have to make the rest of his case against Wittgenstein. He would have to show either that from C-crude it does not follow that this part of our language would be unteachable, or else that it is in fact unteachable, and, of course, it is more likely that he would try the first alternative. But would he succeed?

What is Wittgenstein's own account of our language for sensations in its actual setting? What, indeed, is there left for him to say after he has rejected C-subtle? He has, in fact, two things to say, one of which has received more attention than the other. The thesis which has received more attention is the thesis that a person who understands the meanings of the words that he is using cannot be mistaken in his verbal reactions to his own sensations. This is the negation of the second axiom of C.

It is not altogether easy to see why it should be so essential to Wittgenstein's account that this thesis should be universally true. Obviously there is a lot of truth in it, and this is important. But suppose that there are cases in which the person himself, in spite of being well instructed in the meanings of the appropriate sensation words, might still be mistaken in his verbal reactions to his own sensations. Would this blur the line which Wittgenstein wants to draw between sensations and material objects? It would certainly show that the two are more alike than he was prepared to allow, but not very much more alike. For the speaker need not correct himself by paying more attention to his sensations: it could be pointed out to him, or perhaps he might notice for himself that what he said did not square with the public criteria, and this would not be like what happens when a statement about a material object is corrected, because the language for material objects does not depend in this way on a further auxiliary language. However, if there were cases in which the speaker did correct himself by paying more attention to his sensation, that really would blur Wittgenstein's sharp line. For it would show that statements about sensations sometimes really are much more like statements about material objects than Wittgenstein allows. It would also provide his adversary with the beginnings of an argument against the first version of his demonstration that there could not be a necessarily unteachable language. For he could object that, even if our language for sensations were not only removed from its circle of teaching links, but also entirely segregated from the language for material objects, there would still be a directly verifiable difference between the case in which the speaker really was following a rule for the use of a sensation word, and the case in which he was only under the impression that he was following it. But this objection would have to be made good, and there are several hazards in its way.

Are there in fact any cases in which a person who understands the meanings of the words that he is using might be mistaken, and not merely untruthful in his verbal reactions to his own sensations? In order to establish the answer to this question, Wittgenstein and his adversary would have needed to examine a large range of examples. It would be essential not to concentrate exclusively on the sentence 'I am in pain', which is not the only pebble on this beach. It is obvious that, if there are any counter-examples to Wittgenstein's thesis, they will be found among verbal reactions which are much more specific than this one. Wittgenstein's adversary would formulate the question as a question about knowledge : granted that a learner may not know when he does not know the correct verbal reaction to his sensation, and can be put right by his teacher, is it or is it not the case that, after he has learned the meanings of the words, he will always know the correct verbal reaction to his sensation, or, if he does not know it, will at least know that he does not know it, and so will never make a genuine but unsuccessful attempt to produce the correct verbal reaction? Wittgenstein would not accept this formulation of the question, because it implies that the person may know the correct verbal reaction after he has learned the meanings of the words, whereas, according to him, this phrase is appropriate only before he has learned their meanings. He would formulate the question as a question about ability: granted that a learner may not know when he does not know the correct verbal reaction to his sensation, and can be put right by his teacher, is it or is it not the case that, after he has learned the meanings of the words, he will always be able to produce the correct verbal reaction, so that, if he does not produce it, that will always be because he is being untruthful? This issue will be left at this point.

The second part of Wittgenstein's account of our language for sensations in its actual setting deserves more attention that it usually receives. Anyone who has followed him so far will be puzzled. He is certainly not a behaviourist, because he does not take sensations and other mental phenomena and reduce them without residue to their physical manifestations. Yet he does not accept C-subtle, which tries to keep all the advantages of behaviourism without the paradoxical elimination of the inner life. For he evidently feels that even this theory stands on the slippery slide to error: if we think it out, we shall see that the inner reference must really be completely detachable and dominant, and so the assimilation of sensations to material objects must really be excessive. Naturally, he admits that, when the mind tries to form a view of itself, it has to use a patchwork of physical imagery, because there is nothing else available. But he seems to think that, though there is nothing wrong with the unreflective use of this imagery, yet when we reflect on it we are bound to carry the assimilation of sensations and material objects too far. This is an application of his general theory about the stages by which philosophical understanding is reached. He then tells us at what point we have gone too far and must be retrieved. But to what must we be retrieved? A sensation is something, but what sort of thing is it? There seems to be a vacuum here.

The second part of Wittgenstein's account of our language for sensations is an attempt not to fill the vacuum, but to remove the other's puzzled feeling that there is a vacuum. He does not try to fill it, because to do so would be to produce a philosophical theory about sensations. But he can try to remove the impression that there is a vacuum there by giving a more complete account of the human setting of the language for sensations. For example, we pity people in pain, and, if we can, we try to give them some relief, and, in general, one person's attitude to another is an attitude to a·soul rather than an attitude to an automaton.

This may not satisfy the other. For he may treat the attitude as the sign of a belief, that what is there has a certain character, and so he may ask again for a philosophical specification of the character of what is there when a person is in pain, or has some other kind of sensation. Here the other's reaction is rather like his reaction to Wittgenstein's later treatment of religious propositions. In that case he insisted that the attitude must be based on a factual belief which ought to be specifiable. In this case it is, of course, agreed that the belief that a person is in pain is a factual belief, but the other disagrees with Wittgenstein's treatment of it, because it seems to him to be a mistaken attempt to dissolve the kernel of its factual content into the appropriate attitude.

But at this point Wittgenstein would bring down the guillotine on the debate. If we believe that someone is in pain, we may if we wish describe our belief as the belief that something of a certain kind is there. But if we do describe the belief in this mysterious way, Wittgenstein warns us against supposing that the description can be made more specific in a new philosophical way which will make no reference to the attitude. Either we must go back to the old specification, 'belief that he is in pain', or else, if we want something more, we must go on to the attitude and describe that more thoroughly. There is no hidden source from which a philosopher could draw material for a new kind of specification.

Wittgenstein's idea here is, in a general way, like his main idea about necessity, but there are also differences between the two debates. One general similarity is that in both cases the other wants something more than a full description of the relevant linguistic practices in their actual setting, but in both cases he is given nothing more. Another general similarity is that in both cases the other is the dupe of deceptive pointing. But there is also a difference underlying this second general similarity. For in the first debate he suffered from the illusion that there must be an independent objective backing for logic and mathematics; whereas in this debate his confusion between two areas of discourse seems to point to a new and exciting possibility, which turns out not to be a genuine possibility. This is the difference between the two kinds of deceptive pointing which were distinguished earlier. There is also something else which differentiates the structure of this debate from the structure of the previous one. In the previous one the other wanted a justification of logic and mathematics, but in this one he does not necessarily feel the need for a justification of our language for sensations. Perhaps all he wants is a philosophical specification of the kind of thing that a sensation is. It is, however, quite likely that he will have entered the second debate as a sceptic about other minds, in which case he would be asking for a justification of our language for sensations. So this second difference is not so important as the first difference, between the two kinds of deceptive pointing which are involved. It is a consequence of the first difference that, if Wittgenstein is right in the two debates, it will be in two partly different ways that he is right, and equally so if he is wrong.

9 The True Centre

It is Wittgenstein's later doctrine that outside human thought and speech there are no independent, objective points of support, and meaning and necessity are preserved only in the linguistic practices which embody them. They are safe only because the practices gain a certain stability from rules. But even the rules do not provide a fixed point of reference, because they always allow divergent interpretations. What really gives the practices their stability is that we agree in our interpretations of the rules. We could say that this is fortunate, except that this would be like saying that it is fortunate that life on earth tolerates the earth's natural atmosphere. What we ought to say is that there is as much stability as there is.

This extreme anthropocentrism produces a strange effect on people. They feel that it goes too far, and that it ought to be possible to stop at some earlier point, as Wittgenstein himself had done in the *Tractatus*. But where? It is curiously difficult to relate intermediate theses to his discussions. He moves in to his own solution from the outer extreme with such speed and force that anyone who really starts on the journey with him is likely to go all the way. One of his gifts was extreme far-sightedness, and often he will make a penetrating remark which goes straight through every intermediate position. There is also the spell of his character, and the passionate intensity of his philosophy, which come through very strongly in his writing. Either one is swept along or left behind.

The move to anthropocentrism is associated with a change in his attitude to factual discourse. In the *Tractatus* factual propositions were paid an ambiguous compliment;

they alone had the right to be called 'language'. Whatever their title, they really did have a special connection with the metaphysics of the *Tractatus*. Wittgenstein believed that it was only through a study of their logic that the general structure of reality could be apprehended. It is true that they themselves were supposed to be incapable of describing that structure, but it was through them that this last metaphysical insight could be gained.

It is clear that Wittgenstein was not a destructive positivist. He did not reject all discourse but factual discourse. On the contrary, one of his reasons for plotting the limit of factual discourse was that he wanted to prevent it from encroaching on the others. Nevertheless, factual propositions dominated the scene in a more subtle way, and made their pressure felt beyond their own limits. It was the eminence of factual discourse which forced the others out into the transcendental penumbra. Now it is questionable whether religion, morality and philosophy can exist in that position, and the answer might be different in each of the three cases. But there is no doubt that it is a strange position for them to be in. The simple question, whether the *Tractatus* was a work of destructive positivism or not, has drawn attention away from the strangeness of their position, and from the reason why they were put in it. They were put in it as the result of a comparison with factual discourse, a comparison which, though it was not unfavourable to them, was certainly tough.

However, although in the *Tractatus* he gave one account of factual discourse, and another quite different account of all other kinds of discourse, there was something which, according to him, they all had in common. They all had an independent objective basis outside themselves. This point hardly needed to be made about factual propositions, because they set the standard of objectivity. But he strongly emphasized the objectivity of reality, which, according to him, could be discerned through the logic of factual propositions. He certainly did not then think what he came to think later, that the ontology of the *Tractatus* was merely a projection of a particular way of looking at things. It is true that this ontology, and the theory of language from which it was deduced, could not be expressed in factual propositions. Strictly speaking, it was something which could only be shown, like the truths of morality and religion. But this in no way detracted from the objectivity of these kinds of discourse.

It is difficult to describe the move to anthropocentrism in an accurate and neutral way. Any description of it has to mention the point of departure, which was objectivism, and so there will be the suggestion that things are less secure than we had supposed. This suggestion must be cancelled, if Wittgenstein's position is to be understood. He is not rejecting objectivism and offering a rival theory. The very use of the word 'anthropocentrism' is likely to give the wrong impression, not because it is an inaccurate label, and some other word would be better, but because it instantly places Wittgenstein's view in the arena with its apparent rival, and so it is taken for granted that there will be a philosophical conflict according to the old rules. It is, therefore, essential to remember how different Wittgenstein's intention was. He believed that the correct method was to fix the limit of language by oscillation between two points. In this case the outer point was the kind of objectivism which tries to offer an independent support for our linguistic practices, and the inner point is a description of the linguistic practices themselves, a description which would be competely flat if it were not given against the background of that kind of objectivism. His idea is that the outer point is an illusion, and that the inner point is the whole truth, which must, however, be apprehended through its contrast with the outer point. It is quite correct to apply the word 'anthropocentrism' to the inner point, provided that there is no implication that it is an alternative to objectivism. Wittgenstein's idea is that objectivism, in its only tenable form, collapses into anthropocentrism. It would, therefore, be better to say that there is only one possible theory here, the theory that there is nothing but the facts about the relevant linguistic practices.

The way in which this move to anthropocentrism is associated with the change in Wittgenstein's attitude to factual discourse is less difficult to describe. Looked at from this point of view the move can be broken down into two component moves. First, factual discourse is deprived of its position of eminence, and all the other kinds, except philosophical discourse, are grouped around it on the same level. Secondly, philosophy becomes a special kind of factual investigation. Philosophical propositions state ordinary facts about our linguistic practices and their setting in our lives, but what gives them their point is their background. So all the modes of thought which had been pushed out into the transcendental penumbra are now taken in again and resettled in a more realistic way.

Wittgenstein's early philosophy had been divisive and tolerant: he saw deep gulfs between the various modes of thought, and he believed that the only kind of theory which would cover them all would be a theory which explained how each of them could exist independently in its own appropriate place. His later philosophy retains both these characteristics, but it offers no theory, and it draws a different map. The various modes of thought are placed side by side on the new map, which does not actually show the third dimension. It must be read against a deep background of dream and illusion, but all that it actually shows is the pattern of our linguistic practices. Any philosophical question is to be answered by bringing it down to the level of these facts about language. There is, for example, no independent objective basis which will justify logical inference, and the only possible justification of it is that this is how people think and speak. Hume had treated causal inference in precisely this way, except, of course, that he approached the problem not through language, but through psychology. He maintained that causal inference has no objective external justification, and that its only possible justification is that it is a natural habit of thought. He gave the same kind of answer to the question, what the basis of morality is, and in general his philosophy is a kind of psychological naturalism. Wittgenstein's later philosophy is another species in the same genus: it is not psychological naturalism, but linguistic naturalism. In almost every other way the two philosophers are as different from one another as they could be, but at this point, which is the most important one, there is a striking affinity between them.

This kind of answer to philosophical questions is positivistic. It is not the philistine attitude of rejection which is what is usually meant by 'positivism'. On the contrary, the whole point of answering philosophical questions in this way is that there is no discrimination against any of the modes of human thought. Each is accepted on its own terms, and justified by its own internal standards. But there is another point of view from which this kind of philosophy may be classified as a subtle type of positivism. For what it says is that there is nothing but the facts.

In order to see the difference between this subtle kind of positivism and the usual destructive kind, we have to ask what exactly is being denied by a person who says that there is nothing but the facts. The destructive positivist is denying the significance of all discourse that is not factual: according to him, all other kinds are empty verbiage. This is an extreme position which is seldom occupied, but some philosophers have come near to it. One answer to this kind of positivism is tolerance backed up by general objectivism: each kind of discourse has its own standard of significance, because each has its own independent objective basis. What the subtle kind of positivist is denying is the second half of this answer, the general objectivism. He agrees with the tolerance, but rejects its basis: if there is anything in a particular area of discourse which seems to require justification, then the only possible justification will lie in the facts about the relevant linguistic practices, because there is nothing outside these facts. So the two denials are directed at two different, but connected targets. The destructive positivist is denying the significance of certain kinds of discourse. The subtle positivist claims that they are all significant, but he concedes that some of them contain things which seem to stand in need of justification, and that, if no justification is forthcoming, many will find his claim unconvincing. However, he denies that there is any possibility of justifying them by appealing to anything outside the relevant facts about language, and he makes the further claim that these facts provide all the justification that is needed.

The striking feature of Wittgenstein's anthropocentrism is its generality. There is nothing unusual in the idea that religious beliefs ought not to be assimilated to factual beliefs, and that their meaning is determined by their place in our lives. But it is remarkable that logic should be treated in a similar anthropological way. The new philosophy has an extraordinary levelling effect. It does not assimilate one kind of discourse to another: on the contrary, it is always the differences between them that are emphasized, and particularly the difference between factual discourse and the other kinds. But it does bring all the great philosophical questions which arise within them back to the same level, ordinary human life, from which philosophy started. Philosophy is the voyage out, and the voyage back, both of which are necessary if the logical space of our ordinary linguistic practices is to be understood.

However, though it is true that Wittgenstein's later philosophy has this subtle positivistic character, that is only one side of it. The other side is something quite different. The other side of it is his resistance to the thrust of science, which, he felt, must not be allowed to encroach on other modes of thought. This resistance was a conspicuous feature of his early philosophy, and it continues, in a different form, in the later period. These two tendencies, the resistance to science and the subtle positivism, are not directly opposed to one another, but they are obliquely opposed to one another. His later philosophy is really a resolution of this parallelogram of forces. He never was much concerned with destructive positivism, which probably seemed to him to be not worth consideration. But he was always preoccupied with the pseudo-scientific treatment of religion, morality and philosophy, which sometimes provokes the destructive positivistic reaction.

So on the one hand he rejects the pseudo-scientific treatment of non-factual modes of thought, and he defends their claim to independence. But on the other hand he has to conduct the defence according to the rules of philosophical procedure which he himself believes to be the only possible ones: all that can be done is to present the relevant facts about language.

In the case of religion there was a defence which had already been used by many other thinkers, and which was adopted by Wittgenstein himself in the *Tractatus*. A religious tenet is not a factual hypothesis, but something which affects our thoughts and actions in a different way. This sort of view of religion fits very naturally into his later philosophy: the meaning of a religious proposition is not a function of what would have to be the case if it were true, but a function of the difference that it makes to the lives of those who maintain it. Religious beliefs, unlike scientific beliefs, are not hypotheses, are not based on evidence, and cannot be regarded as more or less probable.[1] So he criticizes Frazer for supposing that religious observances embody

1. The influence of Kierkegaard is very strong at this point. See *Lectures and Conversations on Aesthetics, Psychology and Religious Belief*, ed. Cyril Barrett, Blackwell, 1966, pp. 52–72.

rudimentary scientific insights.[2] Religion and science neither overlap nor conflict with one another.

If there is a definite view of religion in Wittgenstein's later philosophy, this is it. However, it must be pointed out that in this particular area, although he leaves no doubt about what he was rejecting, he is evidently reluctant to put forward any definite view of his own. It might be thought that his reluctance is simply one more aspect of his general refusal to offer philosophical theories, about which more will be said later. But, though it is hard to judge such matters, he does seem to be especially unwilling to accept the subtle positivistic theory of religious belief. On the other hand, he frequently gravitates towards it, certainly does not reject it, and apparently has nothing else to put in its place. So what he withheld, or at least sometimes withheld, was his formal acceptance of it. He had to accept it under protest, but perhaps it was the protest that came from the deeper source. So, although his view of religious belief was anthropocentric, like his view of logic, his feelings about the two predicaments were very different. In the second case he embraced the theory, but that was not what happened in the first case.

It is evident that philosophy, unlike religion, is not a part of ordinary life, but a kind of excursion from it. So it was not possible for Wittgenstein to defend philosophy against the encroachments of science in quite the same way. Of course, the defence would be a piece of descriptive anthropology, and what was described would be a natural tendency of human beings. But philosophizing, however natural it may be, is something outside ordinary life and ideas. It was, therefore, impossible to assume that people understand this mode of thought. It was particularly risky to assume that it is understood, even in a general way, by those who practise it. So in this case the account given by

2. Wittgenstein's criticisms of Frazer's *The Golden Bough* were published in *Synthese*, Vol. 17, No. 3, September 1967.

Wittgenstein might well be utterly surprising to people who had spent their lives philosophizing. The way in which he resolves the parallelogram of forces in this area is extremely complex, and the result is a view of philosophy which is original and fascinating.

When science threatens to encroach on philosophy, his resistance takes a very elaborate form. His first line of defence is his refusal to construct systematic philosophical theories. But behind this there is another line, which is equally important, but very elusive. He believed that the philosopher's presentation of linguistic examples should be like the work of an artist rather than the work of a scientist. But, though it is evident to anyone who reads *Philosophical Investigations* that this is the way in which he saw his work, it is difficult to be sure of the precise points of analogy.

The first line of defence is easier to understand. There are many dangers to which systematic philosophical theories are exposed, but the greatest danger is, paradoxically, that they may not really threaten one another. Although it seems at first that there must be a way of deciding between them, when none is found, the explanation will often be that their apparent incompatibility is a sham. It is then natural to treat them as pictures which seem to point to new possibilities, or to the objective bases of old necessities, but in reality point to nothing. So the confused ideas which have been crowded into these pictures will be separated from one another and methodically hunted to extinction. The other will be led by gradual transitions from something which he does want to say, but which is really, if he could only see it, nonsense, to something else which consistency forces him to say, and which he will immediately recognize as nonsense. This analysis will move slowly from one carefully chosen linguistic example to another, and its purpose will be to retrieve the other. He must be brought back to our actual linguistic practices, and, if he is brought back to them, it will be with an understanding of them which he could not have achieved without his excursion into the dreamworld of language.

Wittgenstein's second line of defence is more elusive. Suppose that someone agreed with his rejection of systematic theorizing in philosophy, but still insisted that, if his linguistic examples do anything at all, this will only be because they can be put into groups which exhibit common characteristics. If this suggestion, which was made in the earlier discussion of his method, is right, it will be impossible to avoid implicit generalizations about the groups of examples and their characteristics. For if there were no such true generalizations, the presentation of the examples would be ineffective. A medicine is made up according to a prescription. Naturally, the implicit generalizations would not need to be as ambitious as systematic theories, but it would be impossible to do without them.

It is uncertain whether Wittgenstein believed this suggestion to be false. He certainly did not think that the idea which it puts forward could be used in philosophy. He may have thought that it is false as well as useless, but it is not entirely clear whether that was his view.

The reason why he believed it to be useless to try to generalize in philosophy was that the subject is too complex. It is really an over-simplification to say that the philosopher produces a map of the space of language, because this suggests that his task is a mechanical one, governed by fixed conventions, and with a fixed standard of completeness. In his Preface to *Philosophical Investigations* Wittgenstein compares the book to an album of sketches made at different points in a long and involved journey. Often the same place is visited many times from different directions, and so there are many different views of it. The philosopher's task is not to impose a uniform grid on the space of language. He is more like an artist who has a deep feeling for a piece of country, and an inexhaustible interest in it, because he grew up in it.

It is possible that, when Wittgenstein stresses the individuality of his linguistic examples, his point is only that
it is useless to try to generalize in philosophy. But he may
also have had something else in mind. Complexity is one
thing, and unanalysable uniqueness is another thing, and it
may be that he thought that the meanings of the things that
people say are irreducibly particular. This is a vague suggestion. How much more precise can it be made?

His feeling for the individuality of the particular case is
certainly reinforced by his holism, which was mentioned in
the earlier discussion of his theory of elementary propositions. It was pointed out there that that theory is not at all
characteristic of his thinking, because it is atomistic,
whereas his tendency is always to see the connections between things and to keep his sense of the totality. Naturally, this tendency plays a recessive role in the atomistic
theory of meaning of the *Tractatus*, but it makes itself felt
whenever he develops the metaphysical consequences of
the theory. In the *Bemerkungen* it comes out clearly in his
revision of the theory of elementary propositions: it was a
mistake to suppose that each elementary proposition gets
its meaning independently of every other, because the truth
is that they come in interrelated groups. For example, a
particular colour proposition ought not to be compared
with a ruler laid against reality: the proper subject of this
comparison is the whole group of colour propositions. It
would be a natural development of this new account of
elementary propositions to say that the meaning of any
proposition is always a function of its place in a larger
whole. This, of course, is what he does say in his later
writings. He does not completely reject the old method of
analysis by paraphrase. But he is always aware of its limitations, and of the need to supplement it with an account of
the surroundings of a particular kind of utterance, and of
its place in our lives. There are also many cases in which he

says that it is impossible either to analyse or to give any general account of what people mean when they use a particular form of words. They mean what they say.

The consequences of atomism and holism are curiously similar. According to the atomistic theory of the *Tractatus* the meaning of an elementary proposition can be apprehended only through acquaintance with the particular objects which it mentions. Uniqueness of meaning is also secured by holism, but in a different way. For if the meaning of a particular proposition is a function of its place in human life and language, it may well be that no two propositions can occupy exactly the same place. So in different ways the two theories would both secure uniqueness of meaning. Atomism leaves comparatively little for the philosopher to say about the meaning of a particular proposition. But holism gives him an enormously complex task: the same place must be approached again and again and all its aspects must be recorded.

There are other ideas which come in at this point, and help to preserve philosophy against the encroachments of science. There is, for example, a connection between this holistic theory of meaning and aesthetics. If someone is listening to a piece of music, and a theme makes a certain impression on him, he may be able to convey the impression to someone else, but not by the kind of analysis and generalization which would be appropriate in science. He is struck by a definite aspect of the theme, but he cannot break it down into distinct components, each with a force that can be assessed in a general way, as in mechanics. He may see its place in the whole work, and about this he will be able to say something, but nothing scientific. Or it may be that he can only proceed by making certain comparisons with other themes, or perhaps, outside music altogether, with ideas and feelings which find a different form of expression.

When Wittgenstein gave this account of aesthetic appreciation,[3] he did not merely regard it as something vaguely similar to understanding the meaning of a particular proposition. He thought that the two things have a definite common factor: both involve the seeing of aspects, and to see an aspect is always to be aware of relations which reach out from the particular case in innumerable directions and give it its unique character.

He also thought that these achievements of the human mind have a certain immunity from scientific analysis. They are examples of psychological attitudes or reactions which are directed towards particular objects. Their intentionality, or 'directedness', does not seem to be analysable as an ordinary relation of a kind that might hold between one physical object and another, and so some philosophers have suggested that it is the distinctive mark of mental phenomena. When Hume tried to devise a kind of mechanics of the mind which would rival Newton's achievement in astronomy, the obvious tool for him to use was the concept of causality, but as the later Phenomenologists pointed out in their criticisms of him, it does not seem to be possible to show that intentionality is really a case of ordinary causality. It is, of course, true that, when someone reacts to an aspect of an object which he sees, the object causes his reaction. But does the statement that his reaction was directed towards a particular aspect of the object mean that there was something about the object which caused it? Even if it does mean this, would it be an ordinary case of causality, governed by general laws? If it were, it ought to be possible to break down the relevant aspect of the object into its various components, and to establish general connections between each of these components and some element in his reaction, as in the mechanical analysis and explanation of impact and movement. But it is not clear how any such thing could be done, and it is arguable that this

3. *Lectures and Conversations on Aesthetics, Psychology and Religious Belief*, pp. 20–21 and 28–9.

whole programme in the philosophy of mind is yet another phase in the mistaken assimilation of mental phenomena to physical phenomena.

It is, of course, questionable whether this part of the assimilation really is mistaken. It may only be that mental phenomena are more complex, and that part of the difficulty is that we are so accustomed to the smooth surface which regular use has put on them, that we feel that their inner complexity is no part of our mental life. But Wittgenstein was always opposed to any such suggestion, and his rejection of this kind of analysis was a constant feature of his philosophy of mind.

There is an interesting example of this opposition in a passage in the *Bemerkungen*, in which he argues against the causal theory of meaning.[4] He points out that cause and effect are connected contingently, but that the connection between a picture or a proposition and the fact which would verify it is a necessary connection, given the intention of the person who uses it. To put his point in a slightly different way, the connection is an inner one, because, if the proposition lacked it, it would not be the same proposition. According to him, this connection cannot be explained by bringing in some third, contingently connected thing, such as the experience of recognition. For someone might use a proposition to signify a particular fact, and later, when he was confronted with another, slightly different fact, he might have the experience of recognition, and so he might come to think mistakenly that this is what he had originally meant. He would settle for a meaning which his original proposition did not have. Similarly, between the expression of a desire and its object there is an inner connection which cannot be explained in the way in which Russell tried to explain it, by bringing in the feeling of satisfaction.[5] For this feeling might be produced by something

4. *Philosophische Bemerkungen*, pp. 63–74.
5. *Analysis of Mind*, Allen and Unwin, first published in 1921. Ch. 3.

which was not the original object of the desire. In the *Conversations on Freud* he makes a similar point.[6] He is criticizing the interpretation of the symbolism of dreams by free association. The person who had the dream may follow a path through the complicated maze of his associations, and this path may lead him to an interpretation of his dream. But, according to Wittgenstein, that does not prove that this is what his dream must have meant, or even that it had any meaning at all.

In these three cases what he is opposing is an analysis of intentionality which relies entirely on a later reaction, supposedly caused in an ordinary way by a later situation. The point of the analysis is that the later reaction not only indicates the object of the original desire or meaning, but is a logically necessary and sufficient condition of the truth of the statement that the person originally desired or meant that thing. Wittgenstein's criticism of this analysis is a strong one. But he also has another objection to it which goes deeper. Even if the analysis were correct as far as it goes, it does not go far enough, because it does not explain the relation between the later reaction and its object. The idea behind the analysis is that this reaction is an undifferentiated effect which is caused in an ordinary way by the later situation. But at this point the analysis simply runs again into all the old difficulties which beset Hume's programme in the philosophy of mind. Would it really be the same reaction if it had a different object? Is it really possible to break down the object into its various components, and to establish a general connection between each component and some element in the reaction? It may only be a mistaken assimilation of mental phenomena to physical phenomena which suggests that these difficulties are not insuperable.

Whatever the solutions to these problems, Wittgenstein's

6. *Lectures and Conversations on Aesthetics, Psychology and Religious Belief*, pp. 41–52.

treatment of them certainly reinforces his resistance to science at a place where it has often threatened to encroach on philosophy. If the mental phenomenon of intentionality really has the autonomy which he claims for it, it would be beside the point to try to analyse the object of a reaction and generalize about it. If philosophy really is like art, the impression made by a linguistic example would be something which could not be caught in any general formula. The particular case would always elude this kind of treatment, because the place which it occupied in the whole system would give it a unique character.

It is not certain how far Wittgenstein really intended to go in this direction. What is certain is that he refused to construct systematic theories, and that instead he tried to fix the limits of logical space by the method of oscillation. Whenever the other strayed into misleading generalities, he had to be brought back to the particular facts about language, which he really knew all the time. Wittgenstein certainly went further than this, but it is not clear exactly how far he went, or precisely what view he took of the appreciation of the particular case.

However, there is no doubt about the force which impelled him in this direction. All his philosophy expresses his strong feeling that the great danger to which modern thought is exposed is domination by science, and the consequent distortion of the mind's view of itself. Although he shared this feeling with Kant, it produced a rather different effect in his case. Kant's reaction to the threat was to produce elaborate systematic defences of the autonomy of religion, morality and philosophy. Wittgenstein's defences of religion and morality are cryptic, inhibited, possibly unhappy and certainly for the most part not original. In his case the most interesting and fully developed result that the feeling produced was his later view of philosophy.

But it is only one half of the truth to say that his resistance to science produced his later view of philosophy.

There was also his linguistic naturalism, which played an equally important role. These two tendencies, one of them anti-positivistic and the other in a more subtle way positivistic, are not diametrically opposed to one another. But there is great tension between them, and his later philosophy is an expression of this tension. Each of the two forces without the other would have produced results of much less interest. The linguistic naturalism by itself would have been a dreary kind of philosophy done under a low and leaden sky. The resistance to science by itself might have led to almost any kind of nonsense. But together they produced something truly great.

Postscript to the Fontana Press Edition

It would be easy to give such a short book a long postscript. So many things were left out, or, if they were mentioned, the opportunities to mark the connections between them were so often missed. However, the additions that I am going to make to what I wrote fifteen years ago will not be numerous, but, as I see it now, they are things that are too important to be passed over again. They come from various sources—the writings of others who have worked on the interpretation of Wittgenstein's philosophy, the reviews of the first edition of this book, and my own further reflections on the texts that I used in 1970 and others that I have read since then.

Solipsism, a minimalist thesis, is a good starting-point. On pages 75–6 and 89–90 I present it as a piece of metaphysics which Wittgenstein did not endorse in the *Tractatus* but which did seem to him to contain a good point. It is not easy to express that point, but perhaps it may be put like this: 'All experience is had from a point of view, which is not represented in the experience itself, but is, as it were, its inner limit. Its outer limit is equally elusive, like the boundary of the visual field, beyond which there is nothing else on the same level.'

What I failed to mention is that Wittgenstein takes up this Schopenhaueresque idea again in 1929, develops it and applies it to the language in which we exchange reports on our sensations. That language is, he might have said, the very devil. The difficulty is to explain how it can be a proper part of the unified language which, according to the *Tractatus*, mirrors the one and only world. It is not too hard to show that the solipsist's field of consciousness cannot be a breakaway world, but it is very hard to integrate it with the physical world without denaturing it, as behaviourists do.

There are really two problems here, one about the objects in a person's field of consciousness and the other about the inner subject or ego. Wittgenstein's discussions of them follow two parallel lines, starting from his treatment of solipsism, which is, therefore, the key to their interpretation.

He argued in the *Tractatus* that, when the solipsist claims that all experiences are had by his ego, he fails to connect his ego with his body and so there is no justification for calling it 'his'. It lacks a criterion of identity and it may just as well be the collective ego of the whole human species—an interpretation which points to idealism rather than solipsism. There is a dilemma here. For if the solipsist does tie his ego to his body, his claim will be self-refuting, because his body is placed in the world among other bodies, each with its own field of consciousness. This shows that the solipsist's field of consciousness cannot be a breakaway world.

The solution to the problem of the ego is implicit in the *Tractatus* but it is worked out in detail in Wittgenstein's early middle period. The ego itself vanishes without our feeling any sense of loss. My field of consciousness, like the field of vision that it contains, is self-authenticating: if a sensation occurs in it, I do not even have to ask myself whose it is. There is no inner owner for me to point at and I may as well drop the word 'I' and say, 'There is pain.' True, this is not really a non-referential theory, because it will mean that there is pain in this field of consciousness, but no reference will be made to an ego. Externally, my body will indicate the owner of the pain simply by being the body from whose mouth the words come. So in my field of consciousness there is no separate owner to point at, while in the physical world, where there is something to point at, there is no need for any pointing, because my body speaks and gesticulates for itself.

The problem about the objects in the solipsist's field of consciousness proved more intractable. Evidently, it needed to be treated in a similar way to the problem of the subject. Sensations, like the subject who has them, needed to be given criteria of identity that would tie them down in the one and only world. They must not be allowed to float away into a transcendental limbo, which is what happens to the ego in solipsism or idealism. On the other hand, they must not be tied down so closely to their physical basis that they are denatured in the way proposed by behaviourism or eliminative materialism.

The problem is a difficult one. It is not enough to give sensations a criterion of numerical identity derived from the identity of their owner. We also need criteria of identity for their various types. When I talk about 'this sensation', I can rely on you to identify me and to realize that it is one that I am now having. But is it a pain or is it some other type of sensation? Here we both need criteria of type-identity. There is only one field of consciousness for each body and in that field individual sensations can be numerically identified by the time of their occurrence, but their types cannot be tied down in such a simple way.

This is not the place to trace all the vicissitudes of the idea behind the treatment of solipsism in the *Tractatus*.[1] There are, however, two connections of thought that are too important to be left unmentioned.

Suppose that the solipsist is not at all complacent about his strange claim, but suffers from anti-Cartesian doubts. What exactly is this ego? All that he can do is to gesture, or, rather, to imagine that he is gesturing in the direction of the focal point behind his field of consciousness. But this achieves nothing if it is not associated with any criterion

1. I shall do that in my forthcoming book, *The False Prison: a Study of the Development of Wittgenstein's Philosophy*, Oxford.

of identity for the ego. Similarly, if he feels doubt about assigning a sensation to a specific type, it is not enough to gesture at its type while saying to himself, 'It is *this* type.' Again, pointing achieves nothing without a criterion of identity.

There is here an important connection of thought. When the solipsist points backwards in the direction of his ego or points forward at his sensation-types, his gestures, or, to be more accurate, his imagined gestures will be empty unless they are associated with viable criteria of identity.

The second connection of thought that needs to be mentioned takes Wittgenstein's philosophy into a higher orbit and it will require a rather longer explanation. But, first, it can be put briefly like this. Informative pointing must involve a certain tension between the apparatus behind the gesture and its target. It is no good strapping the clock-hand down to the dial so that they both go round together (see p. 75). But the need for tension behind informative pointing is only a special case of the general need for tension between language and the world. In fact, it will turn out that the difficult problem about sensation-language, the problem of sensation-types, can be solved only by a theory of language which allows for the necessary tension.

That is a swift sketch of the second connection of thought. In order to get the details, we need to look at Wittgenstein's argument for the impossibility of a private language (pp. 158–9); or, rather, we need to look at *one of his two arguments* for the impossibility of a private language—the other one will be introduced later.

A private language is a necessarily unteachable language. If sensation-types altogether lacked physical and physiological criteria, sensation-language would be necessarily unteachable. But could a person teach himself such a language? Wittgenstein argues that he could not, because, if he had no independent, external criteria for his sensation-types, he would be unable to distinguish between two quite different situations: in one situation he does his best to apply his private word correctly and believes that he is succeeding and he is right, and in the other situation everything is exactly the same as far as he can tell, but he is wrong. But it is essential that he should be able to tell the difference between these two situations. How else could he acquire proficiency? More radically, how could there *be a proficiency* to be acquired?

Two people draw a target in the sand and throw stones at it, a competitive game with a visible criterion of success. Of course, they need not actually draw the target in the sand: they could use a map showing its exact position on the beach. But now suppose that the one who has the map refuses to let the other one see it. Then, though there is a proficiency to be acquired, the one who is kept in the dark about the position of the target is not in a position to acquire it. Finally suppose that the secretive player simply defines the target as 'wherever my shots fall'. In that case there is no proficiency to be acquired. The necessary tension between the operation and the target has collapsed. He has defined the target in terms of his best attempt to hit it and his subjective impression that he is hitting it. But what then is *it*? How can there even be an attempt to do something without any independent criterion of doing it successfully?

This was Wittgenstein's objection to a sensation-language which is necessarily unteachable because there are no external criteria for its sensation-types: nobody could even teach himself such a language, because there would be nothing to learn, no proficiency to be acquired. The necessary tension between language and the world would have collapsed, just like the necessary tension between informative pointing and its target. He is, of course, attacking the kind of account of sensation-language that can be found in Russell's writings and in the long tradition behind them: first, it is said, we teach ourselves sensation-language in complete independence of everything physiological and physical, and then we have to regain our foothold in the external world.

However, though this was Wittgenstein's main objection to treating sensations as private objects, he must have believed that there is something else wrong with this kind of philosophical theory. Otherwise he would have accepted the account of sensation-language which Carnap gave in 1935 (see p. 153). But there is no doubt that he did not accept it, and his reasons are discussed in the second half of Chapter 8, rather inconclusively, as it now seems to me.

I shall not try to improve that discussion now, because there is something more important to be done. Barry Stroud in his review of this book,[2] pointed out that I said very little about the great investigation of rule-following which is the centre of Wittgenstein's later theory of meaning, and that what I did say was not brought to bear on the questions about sensation-language that have just been raised. True, and I want to take this opportunity to put that right.

There are two quite different views that might be taken of what I omitted. One view would be that the difficulties that I experienced in interpreting Wittgenstein's main objection to treating sensations as private objects vanish in the light of what he says about rule-following. The extreme version of this view can be found in Kripke's powerfully argued book.[3] He was the first to suggest that the examination of the special problems of sensation-language, which starts at § 243 of *Philosophical Investigations*, can only be understood in the light of the

2. *Journal of Philosophy*, Vol. LXIX, no. 1, pp. 16–26, 1972.
3. Saul Kripke, *Wittgenstein on Rules and Private Language*, Basil Blackwell, 1982.

discussion of rule-following that precedes it. That is the moderate version of the view. The extreme version contains the claim that what I call 'Wittgenstein's main objection to treating sensations as private objects' is not really that at all, but only a corollary of conclusions reached in the preceding discussion of rule-following.

The other view that might be taken of this matter is that Wittgenstein has two private language arguments, one developed before § 243 of *Philosophical Investigations* and the other after it. The first argument, which Kripke chooses for the role of *the* private language argument, is not concerned with the special problems of sensation-language but with the general analysis of rule-following; while the second argument, which all interpreters of *Philosophical Investigations* chose for the unique role before reading Kripke's book, and which some still try to maintain in that role even after reading it, is not concerned with the general analysis of rule-following but only with the special problems of sensation-language.

I shall now argue for the second view. If my arguments are valid, they will establish that the account given in this book of Wittgenstein's main objection to treating sensations as private objects is substantially correct but superficial. If we go into the matter more deeply, we shall see that Wittgenstein's second private language argument is derived from the fundamental premiss that there must be tension between language and the world. We shall also see that his first private language argument is derived from the same source. So the reinstatement of what I originally omitted at this point will put us on the road to discovering the deep structure of Wittgenstein's later philosophy.

The difficult thing is to grasp the relation between Wittgenstein's first private language argument and his second one. Let us go back to the second argument and try to get a picture of its structure. In the third version of the game played on the beach one of the players makes a move which may be called 'attaching the target to the gun'. He defines the target entirely in terms of events at his end of the shooting-range. This produces the loss of tension that has been identified as the analogue of the loss of tension between sensation-language and sensations in theories which detach sensations from all physical and physiological criteria. It is also possible to use a mechanical analogy at this point, as Wittgenstein often does, and to say that there must be friction between language and the world, but that all friction is lost when sensations are detached from the external world, because in that situation trying to describe them would be like trying to walk on a conveyor-belt moving at the same speed in the opposite direction.

The question is, 'How is this structure related to the structure of the first private language argument?' Perhaps the adversary whom Wittgenstein is opposing in his first argument is someone who loses the tension between language and the world in the opposite way, by attaching the gun to the target. This would mean that, instead of defining the target in terms of his use of his equipment, he defines his equipment and his use of it in terms of the target.

This will immediately strike some people as an apt description of the kind of theory of meaning that is under attack in the sections preceding § 243 in *Philosophical Investigations*. If this impression is correct, we have a new understanding of the structure of Wittgenstein's later theory of meaning. Tension between language and the world is the fundamental requirement and there are two symmetrical ways in which it can be lost: some theories of sensation-language attach the target to the gun and some theories about descriptive language in general attach the gun to the target.

Support for this interpretation of Wittgenstein's later theory of meaning can be found in the fact that his first private language argument is concerned with any kind of descriptive language, while his second one is concerned only with sensation-language. Naturally. Shooting has its general problems but special problems are presented by certain kinds of target. However, this will hardly be enough to establish such a novel interpretation. What is needed is a detailed examination of the texts, but I have space only for a summary.[4]

Kripke argues not only that what I am calling 'Wittgenstein's first private language argument' is *the* private language argument, but also that it presents a paradox which is inherent in the use of descriptive language. The paradox is that, when someone applies a word to a thing, the meaning with which he uses the word is not anchored in any contemporary fact about him. However, the text of *Philosophical Investigations* will not bear this interpretation. In his first private language argument Wittgenstein is not tackling a paradox inherent in rule-following but pointing out that a certain theory of meaning leads to a paradox. His argument is reductive. The theory under attack is defended by an adversary who may be called 'The Champion of Law and Order', because he maintains that, if there were no more to rule-following than Wittgenstein allows, the disciplined use of language would collapse. Wittgenstein retorts that, on the contrary, the collapse is a consequence of his adversary's theory.

This sounds like the kind of argument that people have in bars late in the evening's drinking. Wittgenstein and his adversary castigate each other's theory in more or less the same words. How can they both have intelligible points? But that is easily explained. Wittgenstein claims that the right way to follow a rule is the way in which we all find it natural to follow it, and he argues that, if we try to nail

4. The details will be given in my forthcoming book, see p. 187, footnote 1.

down our interpretation of the rule in a formula, then the right way to apply the formula will again be the way in which we all find it natural to apply it.

The Champion of Law and Order objects that, if that were true, there would be a free for all and each language-user would just do his own thing. Wittgenstein's reply to this is that it is logically impossible to get from any rule such complete and absolute guidance that those who are following it do not need to make any contribution to what counts as obedience. Of course, this is precisely what worries the Champion of Law and Order, but Wittgenstein's point is that his anxiety leads him to replace the real but incomplete guidance actually provided by rules with a complete but unreal guidance which is an aspiration of fantasy.

Wittgenstein began to develop this Rousseauesque line of thought in 1930, but it did not immediately converge with the later developments of his treatment of solipsism. At first, he merely added it to the picture theory of propositions, which had relied totally on names, but in which the problem of reidentification according to rule had not even come up for discussion. Later, the unusable part of the analogy between propositions and pictures was phased out and then the finished account of rule-following joined forces with the ideas that originated in the *Tractatus* critique of solipsism. In *Philosophical Investigations* the two lines of thought run parallel to one another.

The next step is to explain why Wittgenstein believed that the complete, but unreal guidance which the Champion of Law and Order hoped to get from rules would eliminate the essential tension between language and the world. This is not easy to explain. The difficulty is a special case of the general difficulty of imagining something logically impossible. For Wittgenstein's claim is that what his adversary's theory demands is logically impossible, because a language that satisfied his requirements would lose its tension with the world and cease to be a language.

The logical impossibility that Wittgenstein has in mind needs to be explained with care. The Champion of Law and Order wants rules to give complete and absolute guidance. His idea is that the rule-follower must be able to see in the rule itself the correct answer to the question whether to apply or withhold the word governed by it. He wants this insight to be provided for every situation in which the question could arise, and to be provided without any contribution from the rule-follower himself. It is, of course, granted that his will has to cooperate in the making of the correct move, but the idea is that his intellect must contribute nothing to determining what the correct move is.

Now the rule-follower's mind cannot very well be a blank, and the Champion of Law and Order needs to say what is in it. His suggestion is that what occurs in his mind is always a complete labour-saver, or, rather, a complete mind-sparer. Maybe he has an image, which somehow prefigures all the possible correct applications of the word. Or perhaps the potent talisman is a self-applying formula, or even a flash of understanding which anticipates every predicament together with the appropriate reaction to it.

It is at this point that Wittgenstein's argument makes its impact on his adversary's theory. It is logically impossible that anything in the rule-follower's mind should be a substitute for the unavoidable leap from language to the world. There is no conceivable mental talisman that could take him across his bridges before he comes to them. The correct solutions to his future problems cannot possibly be contained in anything that is in his mind now.

Wittgenstein is not just arguing that the rule-follower's future moves cannot be completely prefigured in his mind. He is making this point about any further moves of his that would actually be correct. He is opposing the idea that what the rule-follower, or community of rule-followers have said or thought in the past lays down fixed rails for what they *ought to say* in the future. His argument is that the very idea is incoherent, because it leads to a paradox.

What still remains to be explained is the way in which Wittgenstein imagines the logically impossible situation required by the Champion of Law and Order. This will bring us at last to the connection between his reductive argument and his fundamental axiom of tension between language and the world.

Someone who sets out to imagine the unimaginable will always choose the point of least resistance presented by the logical impossibility. In this particular case Wittgenstein supposes that the situation in which his adversary's theory would come true would have to be one in which the rule-follower's mental talisman was defined in terms of what he ought to say in the future. This move is supposed to secure the advantage of putting something genuinely contemporary in his mind without the disadvantage of leaving anything for him to contribute to its interpretation. If, for example, the talisman were an image, its meaning would be given by an anticipatory, general, ostensive definition attaching it to the imagined fixed rails of its future correct applications.

This is, of course, absurd, and the absurdity consists in attaching the gun to the target. The rule-follower's training has put him in a state in which he finds it natural to go on and apply the word to this object and withhold it from that one. The Champion of Law and Order emphasizes the importance of this state, but in his anxiety to secure complete guidance he goes too far. He detaches the rule-follower's mental equipment from its actual basis in the present and attaches it by definition to what he ought to say in the future.

Instead of real, but incomplete guidance, this theory offers guidance which is complete but totally unreal.

According to Wittgenstein the distinction between following a rule and violating it can not be wholly independent of the difference between the way in which we find it natural to develop the series and other ways of developing it. If our contribution to what counts as the correct development is obliterated by an anticipatory, general, ostensive definition, the necessary tension between language and the world is lost. The rule-follower's language becomes private, not because nobody else can get the hang of what he is doing, but because he is not *doing* anything.

Wittgenstein was trained as an engineer and he uses mechanical analogies rather than the analogy of shooting when he is presenting his two private language arguments. In his reductive argument against the theory of the Champion of Law and Order he includes a discussion of 'the machine as symbol', and a thorough examination of his argument would need to show why a machine which seems to anticipate its own future performance is such an apt illustration of the point in his adversary's theory that is under attack. It would also be necessary to examine his mechanical analogue for the theory of sensation-language against which his second private language argument is directed. I used the analogy of a man trying to walk on a conveyor-belt moving at the same speed in the opposite direction, but he uses a different mechanical analogy.

There is also another gap which still remains to be filled in the exposition of Wittgenstein's second private language argument. It is clear that it is directed against any theory of sensation-language that detaches sensations from their external criteria and from their place in human life. But what exactly are the resources that are discounted by that kind of theory? The resource that has received most attention in recent discussions of Wittgenstein's positive doctrine is agreement in judgements with other people. But there is also quite a lot of evidence that he believed that a rule-follower operating on his own could rely on standard objects for the calibration of his reactions.

The structure of Wittgenstein's thought which emerges even in a brief account of his later philosophy is impressive. There is an elegant symmetry in the relationship between the two private language arguments and an underlying similarity, to which he draws attention in unpublished work, between the ego's relation to the world and language's relation to the world. These are, of course, abstract features of his thought, but even in his most detailed investigations their guiding force can always be felt.

I can illustrate this by mentioning one more connection of thought that I missed when I wrote this book. It is a corollary of the *Tractatus* theory of meaning that possibilities and necessities can only be shown in the logical grammar of language. We can never look through the logical grammar and perceive any independent, supporting facts beneath it. True, our acceptance of necessities and possibilities is not arbitrary, but it is not founded on the independently describable natures of things. I did mention this (e.g. on p. 103 and on p. 132) and I explained that it is as important in his later work as it was in the *Tractatus*. But I failed to mention its connection with the main result of his investigation of rule-following.

The main result is that, though the way in which we find it natural to continue a series is not arbitrary, it has no independent foundation in the world. This is, in a certain sense, a non-theory. It is beyond realism and idealism and it yields a modified account of the things which, according to the *Tractatus*, can only be shown, not said. They are things that manifest themselves in the ways in which we find it natural to speak, given our previous linguistic acts. This is the special mode in which, as he says in *Zettel*, 'nature makes herself audible'.

Biographical Note

Ludwig Wittgenstein was born in Vienna in 1889. After leaving school at the age of 17 he went to Berlin to study engineering. In 1908 he went to England, and after a few months registered as a research student in the department of engineering at Manchester University. His research was in aeronautics. In 1912 he was admitted to Trinity College Cambridge to study the foundations of mathematics and logic with Bertrand Russell. During the war he served in the Austrian army. He finished writing the *Tractatus Logico-Philosophicus* in 1918. The German text was published in 1921 in Ostwald's *Annalen der Naturphilosophie*, and in 1922 it appeared in England with an English translation printed opposite the German. He published one other philosophical work in his lifetime, and that was an article. His other major philosophical works have been, and still are being published posthumously (see Bibliography, p. 187). Between 1920 and 1926 he taught in various village schools in Austria. His discussions with the philosophers of the Vienna Circle began in 1927. He returned to Cambridge in 1929, and held a fellowship at Trinity College from 1930 to 1935. In 1939 he was elected professor of philosophy in the University of Cambridge. During the war he was a porter in a London hospital, and later he worked in a medical laboratory in Newcastle. He resigned his chair at Cambridge in 1947. He died in 1951.

A detailed account of his life is given by G. H. von Wright in his *Biographical Sketch*. Norman Malcolm's *Memoir* covers the years 1938 to 1951. These two biographical works were published in 1958 by the Oxford University Press in the same volume, *Ludwig Wittgenstein:*

Wittgenstein

*A Memoir by Norman Malcolm, with a Biographical Sketch
by G. H. von Wright.* Paul Engelmann's *Memoir* covers a
period which begins soon after the outbreak of war and
extends into the 1920s when Wittgenstein was still in Austria : *Letters from Ludwig Wittgenstein, with a Memoir :*
Paul Engelmann : translated by L. Furtmüller and edited
by B. F. McGuinness : Basil Blackwell, Oxford, 1967.

Short Bibliography

Part 1 is based mainly on the following two works :–

Tractatus Logico-Philosophicus, L. Wittgenstein, German with English translation by C. K. Ogden and F. P. Ramsey, with an introduction by B. Russell, Routledge and Kegan Paul, London, 1922: German with English translation by D. F. Pears and B. F. McGuinness, with B. Russell's introduction, Routledge and Kegan Paul, London, and Humanities Press, New York, 1961.

Notebooks, 1914–16, L. Wittgenstein, German with English translation by G. E. M. Anscombe, edited by G. H. von Wright and G. E. M. Anscombe, Basil Blackwell, Oxford, Harper and Row, New York, 1961. This volume also contains Wittgenstein's *Notes on Logic* (September 1913), his *Notes Dictated to G. E. Moore in Norway* (April 1914), and extracts from his letters to Russell (1912–1920).

Wittgenstein's early notes throw light on many of the more obscure passages of the *Tractatus*. There is also a later work which makes it easier to understand his brief and cryptic treatment of ethics in the *Tractatus* :–

Lecture on Ethics, L. Wittgenstein, which was read to a society in Cambridge in 1929 or 1930, and has been published in the *Philosophical Review*, Vol. LXXIV No. 1, January 1965.

Part 2 is based mainly on the following three works :–

Philosophische Bemerkungen, L. Wittgenstein, German (without English translation) edited by R. Rhees, Basil Blackwell, Oxford, 1964. This work was written in 1929 and 1930.

Philosophical Investigations, L. Wittgenstein, German with English translation by G. E. M. Anscombe, Basil Blackwell, Oxford, Macmillan Co, New York, 1953; 2nd edition (revised), Basil Blackwell, Oxford, 1958.

Remarks on the Foundations of Mathematics, L. Wittgenstein, German with English translation by G. E. M. Anscombe, edited by G. H. von Wright, R. Rhees and G. E. M. Anscombe, Basil Blackwell, Oxford, Macmillan Co, New York, 1956.

The first of these three works belongs to the period of transition from Wittgenstein's early philosophy to his later philosophy. There is another work which belongs to this period and which serves as a comparatively easy introduction to his later philosophy:—

The Blue and Brown Books, L. Wittgenstein, Basil Blackwell, Oxford, 1958. These are notes dictated by Wittgenstein in English.

When other works are mentioned in the text, details of publication etc. are given in footnotes.

Published work on Wittgenstein's philosophy is already voluminous. There are three useful collections of essays by various authors:—

Essays on Wittgenstein's Tractatus, edited by Irving M. Copi and Robert W. Beard, Routledge and Kegan Paul, London, 1961.

Wittgenstein, The Philosophical Investigations, edited by George Pitcher, in the series *Modern Studies in Philosophy*, under the general editorship of Dr Amélie Rorty, Doubleday and Co, New York, 1966.

Ludwig Wittgenstein, the Man and His Philosophy, edited by K. T. Fann, Dell Publishing Co, New York, 1967.

All three of these collections contain bibliographies of Wittgenstein's works and of works by others on Wittgenstein's philosophy. G. H. von Wright's complete survey of Wittgenstein's surviving philosophical papers, including those which have not been published, appeared in the *Philosophical Review*, Vol. LXXVIII No. 4, October 1969.

There are also two general accounts of Wittgenstein's philosophy which have appeared since the publication of the first edition of this book:—

Wittgenstein, Anthony Kenny, Penguin, London, 1973.

An Approach to Wittgenstein's Philosophy, Derek Bolton, Macmillan, London, 1979.

Fontana Modern Masters
Editor: Frank Kermode

Einstein
Second Edition

Jeremy Bernstein

Future generations may well refer to the first half of the twentieth century as 'The Age of Einstein' – so outstanding was his contribution to modern thought. In this book Jeremy Bernstein approaches his career through the three basic themes in his work: the special theory of relativity, the general theory of relativity and gravitation, and the quantum theory. Studying these, the author traces the stages of both Einstein's own life in science and the growth of modern scientific awareness. His account is both lucid and evocative, and goes a long way towards helping the layman to a fuller understanding of Albert Einstein and the central issues of modern physics.

'Jeremy Bernstein's book is good value for money; it devotes itself to an attempt to translate the scientific theories into a more mundane and ambiguous language. Biographical details occupy only a small fraction of the contents, but present the essential elements of Einstein's professional career.'   *Economist*

'Bernstein concentrates on Einstein's physics, ably relating it to the immediate pre-Einsteinian situation, and to its spectacular confirmation.'   *Times Literary Supplement*

Fontana Press

Fontana Modern Masters
Editor: Frank Kermode

Marx

David McLellan

Since his death in 1883, Marx has been revised, distorted and rediscovered. But as David McLellan shows, recent research and scholarship have provided the documentation and perspective that are enabling a more coherent picture to emerge.

This essay is a survey of Marx's life, of his contribution to the varied fields of history, economics and politics, and of his subsequent interpreters by a writer whose own studies have played a major part in fostering this process of redefinition.

'A really first-class, clear-cut and highly articulate commentary ... an example of that rare breed, the successful encapsulation.'
Anthony Masters, *Birmingham Post*

'Hats off to Mr McLellan for taking up only eighty-one pages in reciting the basic notions of *Capital* and *The Communist Manifesto*, while finding room *en route* for the information that the Marx family went regularly for Sunday picnics on Hampstead Heath.'
Robert Nye, *Scotsman*

'McLellan's ninety pages on Marx are a triumph of concentrated exposition.'
Gabriel Pearson, *Guardian*

'An ideal introduction to Marx.'
Richard Geary, *Times Higher Educational Supplement*

Fontana Press

Fontana Modern Masters
Editor: Frank Kermode

Chomsky
Third Edition

John Lyons

Chomsky's contribution to the study of language has, over the last four decades, been enormous, and has influenced those working in many disciplines, including the other cognitive sciences. Language is, arguably, an even more distinctively human characteristic than intelligence, and the thousands of different human languages are, according to Chomsky, cut to the same general pattern. This pattern is determined, he claims, by innate structuring principles which only human beings possess. Chomsky's search for the universal in language has revitalized the question of the relationship between language and mind, and has provided a powerful new tool, generative grammar, for students of language.

In this Third Edition of his concise, accessible introduction to Chomsky's work, John Lyons has added an extensive final chapter which seeks to assess the continuing ramifications of the Chomskyan Revolution in linguistics today. He has also thoroughly updated the bibliographies – both of Chomsky's own prolific output and of the multiplying secondary material – and the biographical note, in order fully to arm any prospective explorer of Chomsky's *oeuvre* with all the relevant resources they may need.

'John Lyons' book on Chomsky is simply the best short introduction in the English language. It is within the grasp of an intelligent layman. Anyone who reads it will understand the elements of transformational grammar, and be able to follow current controversies.'

Leonard Jackson, *Times Educational Supplement*

'Lyons' account is itself a minor modern masterpiece of compression and clarity.'

Alan Ryan, *New Society*

Fontana Press

Fontana Modern Masters
Editor: Frank Kermode

Foucault

J. G. Merquior

'I have never been a Freudian, I have never been a Marxist and I have never been a structuralist.' Michel Foucault

Michel Foucault wanted to defy categorization; he wanted to institute a new order of learning and thinking. When he died, still in his prime, in June 1984, he had already earned the nickname 'the new Sartre'. By attempting a highly original and daring merger of philosophy and history, he had set out to revitalize Western philosophy with bold, provocative theses on our attitudes to madness, the assumptions of science and language, our systems of punishment and discipline, and our ideas about sex. Finally, he presented new perspectives on the phenomenon of power and its relationship with knowledge.

J. G. Merquior's is an uninhibited critical assessment of Foucault as 'a historian of the present'. Encompassing all his published work and an impressive array of secondary literature about Foucault, it appraises his philosophical history and his debts to previous thinkers such as Bachelard and Kuhn, and sketches his complex relationship to French structuralism. It closes with an outline of Foucault's ideological profile as a Nietzschean master of the neo-anarchist mood, and raises important queries as to the ultimate value and legitimacy of his kind of philosophical rhetoric, with its attendant view of the role of the modern intellectual. As more people come to grapple with what Foucault *means*, with his true worth, Merquior's incisive, sane introduction will become indispensable.

Fontana Press